isn't just for holy men; it's for any believer who will reach out in faith, obedience, and sincerity to Him—including you.

God bless you as you read and may God's amazing energy and power flow through you!"

—Dr. Jesse Duplantis ⋎ Jesse Duplantis Ministries

Fast-paced, brief, and riveting, *Anointing for Healing* is a good resource for anyone seeking to build their faith in this area, and the gift-book format also makes it ideal for gift giving. Recommend, too, for stocking in church libraries.

—CBA Retailers & Resources

I have been associated with Gina for many years. What a teacher, what an author, what a friend. A great man of God spoke by the Spirit of God that in the last days, people would so understand the Word of God that it would be like a formula. This book is the "how to." It has much teaching through wonderful testimonies as well as impartations. I truly love it...it's a must for your faith library.

—Lynne Hammond ⋎ Mac Hammond Ministries

You may have to put aside what you have been taught about healing up to now. This inspiring and life-changing book will revolutionize your thinking and faith. If you need a miracle for yourself or a loved one, you are holding it!

—Pamela J. Bolen ⋎ Licensed Professional Counselor

ANOINTING *for*
HEALING

MELANIE HEMRY & GINA LYNNES

ANOINTING FOR HEALING

ISBN: 978-0-88368-687-4
Printed in the United States of America
© 2007 by Melanie Hemry and Gina Lynnes

Whitaker House
1030 Hunt Valley Circle
New Kensington, PA 15068
www.whitakerhouse.com

Library of Congress Cataloging-in-Publication Data

Hemry, Melanie, 1949–
    Anointing for healing / Melanie Hemry and Gina Lynnes.
        p. cm.
    Summary: "Demonstrates the healing power of God through many
miraculous testimonies and the significance of the use of anointing oil
for healing"—Provided by publisher.
    ISBN 978-0-88368-687-4 (hardcover : alk. paper) 1. Spiritual
healing. 2. Holy oils. I. Lynnes, Gina, 1954– II. Title.
        BT732.5.H44 2007
        234'.131—dc22
                                    2007016889

2 3 4 5 6 7 8 9 / 14 13 12 11 10 09

CONTENTS

Frankincense & Myrrh, two of the three prophetic gifts given to the Messiah at His birth, represent prayer, healing, and intercession, signifying all that Messiah would do and continues to do on our behalf.

THE
ANCIENT SYMBOL
THAT NEVER
GROWS OLD

BY GINA

THE ANCIENT SYMBOL THAT NEVER GROWS OLD

Anointing oil. If you think it seems oddly out of place on the cover of a contemporary Christian book, you might just be right. In an age where the church is striving above all to be culturally relevant, anointing oil is...well, definitely not that. In fact, most people would say it's just the opposite: a dusty relic from centuries gone by that should be stashed in an attic trunk nestled next to grandmother's dog-eared King James Bible, not perched on the shelves of a popular bookstore.

So why use it? In this day of multi-media savvy readers who pick up prayer alerts on the Internet and download the latest Christian tunes onto their MP3 players, why stick with a symbol so peculiar and old fashioned?

Because there's no substitute for it.

Anointing oil threads and sparkles its way through the pages of the Bible unlike any other spiritual symbol. From Genesis to the New Testament epistles, it appears again and again, carrying life-changing messages.

Spanning not just centuries but millennia, it has proven to be a spiritual picture worth a thousand words.

Although the words *anoint*, *anointed*, and *anointing* appear more than 150 times in Scripture, and are derived from the Latin word *inunctus*, meaning "smear with oil," anointing oil by itself possesses no mystical properties. It's not magic. It's not even supernatural. Anointing oil cannot heal or deliver or change us at all. The physical application of it alone cannot help us any more than a sermon preached to us in a foreign language. With the oil, as with the sermon, we experience its power only when we understand its message.

What then, is the message of the anointing oil?

It depends on the situation you're facing.

When it first appears in Genesis 28, anointing oil says God is present. He is here right now to protect and provide for all your needs. At least, that is the essence of its meaning there. To see the fullness of its message, we must read the story that surrounds it.

We must see Jacob—lonely and wandering, banished from home, hated by his brother and haunted by his past, sleeping under the stars with his head resting uneasily on a stony pillow. We must dream with him of a heavenly ladder crowded with angels climbing up and down, bringing to earth the blessings Jacob ached to possess. We must hear God's voice hammering the point home and saying, "*Behold, I am with you and will keep you wherever you go...I will not leave you until I have done what I have spoken to you*" (verse 15).

That night, that dream, and that divine voice changed Jacob's life. He wanted to make sure he never forgot those things. So "*Jacob rose early in the morning, and took the stone that he had put at his head, set it up as a pillar, and poured oil on top of it. And he called the name of the place Bethel*" (verses 18–19).

The Hebrew word *Bethel* means "house of God." Think of it! God proved through Jacob's experience that He meets His people in the most stony, desolate seasons of life and pours out His blessings on them. He makes His home with them and promises He will never leave them.

If that had been the only message anointing oil ever preached, the practice of using it would have been worth preserving, but that was just the beginning. In the book of Exodus, anointing oil speaks of holiness and dedication to the Lord. Poured on the priests and splashed around the tabernacle, it declared, "These people and these things belong to God and God alone. They are set apart for His glory."

In the book of Samuel, the anointing oil says, "This person has been chosen by God to reign as a king." It takes a simple young shepherd boy named David and marks him as a royalty. Dripping onto the ruddy cheeks of the totally unknown and unlikely ruler, it proclaims, "This is the one who will trample the enemies of the Almighty under his feet."

In the book of Isaiah, anointing oil preaches a message of deliverance from bondage and freedom from the oppressor. It promises *that his burden will be taken away from your shoulder, and his yoke from your neck, and the yoke will be destroyed because of the anointing oil"* (Isaiah 10:27).

In 2 Chronicles 28:15, the anointing oil speaks of the refreshing and restoration God provides. In Psalm 23, it assures His people that God will honor and exalt them before their enemies like an honored guest. In Psalm 105, it proclaims God's fierce and unfailing protection and says of the children of Israel. "*He permitted no one to do them wrong; yes, He rebuked kings for their sakes, saying, 'Do not touch My anointed ones, and do My prophets no harm'*" (verses 14–15).

ROAD SIGNS TO THE NEW COVENANT

"But those are all Old Testament messages," someone might argue. "Do they really apply to Christians today?"

Yes! In fact, they apply more surely to us than to the people who first received them. "*They were written for our admonition, upon whom the ends of the ages have come*" (1 Corinthians 10:11). Every time anointing oil was used under the old covenant, it pointed forward to the new. Like a sign along the highway, it alerted spiritual travelers to their ultimate destination, to a time when Jesus would open the door for the Holy Spirit to be poured out like anointing oil on all who believed in Him. All through the Old Testament, the anointing oil was preaching about the *Christ*!

Many believers today don't realize it but the very word *Christ* practically shimmers with anointing oil because it literally means *the anointed one*. No wonder Jesus began His ministry on earth by declaring:

> *The Spirit of the LORD is upon Me, because He has anointed Me to preach the gospel to the poor; He has sent Me to heal the brokenhearted, to proclaim liberty to the captives and recovery of sight to the blind, to set at liberty those who are oppressed; to proclaim the acceptable year of the LORD.*
>
> (Luke 4:18–19)

Every glistening drop of anointing oil administered by believers today speaks about Jesus. It declares that because of the blood He shed and the Holy Spirit He has poured out upon us:

- His presence is here with us and in us, transforming each one of us into little Bethels, mobile dwelling places of God.

- We belong to God and God alone. Like the Old Testament priests and tabernacle, we are set apart for His glory, "*a chosen race, a royal priesthood, a dedicated nation, [God's] own, purchased, special people that we may set* forth the wonderful deeds and display the virtues and perfections of Him who called us out of darkness into His marvelous light" (1 Peter 2:9 AMP).

- We have been given the divine authority and power to reign as kings in life through the One Man Jesus Christ. (See Romans 5:17 AMP.)

- We have been freed from the devil's oppression and honored with every spiritual blessing in heavenly places. (See Ephesians 1:3.)

- We are no longer slaves but more than conquerors through Him who loved us. (See Romans 8:37.)

Those messages are powerful all by themselves, yet they are enhanced even further when biblical fragrances are added because each scent symbolizes an aspect of our Savior. Frankincense, one of the gifts presented to Jesus at His birth, represents the call on His life as intercessor. Myrrh represents His purification and preparation—Jesus was anointed with myrrh and aloe for his burial. Pomegranate represents the fruitfulness, abundance, blessing, and favor that Jesus offers. The lily of the valley represents His honor and purity of heart.

Such fragrances have special significance for us as the body of Christ today. Paul revealed why in 2 Corinthians 2:14–16 when he wrote:

> But thanks be to God! For through what Christ has done, he has triumphed over us so that now wherever we go he uses us to tell others about the Lord and to spread the Gospel like a sweet perfume. As far as God is concerned there is a sweet, wholesome fragrance in our lives. It is the fragrance of Christ within us, an aroma to both the saved and the unsaved all around us. To those who are not being saved, we seem a fearful smell of death and doom, while to those who know Christ we are a life-giving perfume. (TLB)

In the light of those verses, we see that all the sweet fragrances in the Old Testament point not only to Jesus but to us. They also represent our prayers, which Revelation 5:8 tells us are lifted in heaven to God as "*golden bowls full of incense.*" What a picture that is: God Almighty breathing into Himself the fragrant prayers of His anointed people, then breathing back out again the answers to those prayers!

That is the picture painted by anointing oil. Once we see it, we can understand why the first twelve disciples used that symbol when they ministered to the multitudes in Jesus' name. We can grasp, even with our contemporary Christian minds, why they *"anointed with oil many who were sick, and healed them"* (Mark 6:13).

Suddenly the instructions in James 5:14 no longer sound odd and archaic. *"Is anyone among you sick? Let him call for the elders of the church, and let them pray over him, anointing him with oil in the name of the Lord."* In the light of what that oil has preached to God's people through the ages, it's easy to imagine how the heart of an ailing saint who understood its message might leap with joy as that oil touched his skin. We can almost hear its sermon thundering in his ears, declaring that the burden-removing, yoke-destroying power of Jesus Himself has been released in his body. The One anointed to heal...and deliver...and honor...and protect...and bring victory is here!

That, in essence, is the message of anointing oil. Whether or not the symbol is culturally relevant may be up for debate. But one thing is indisputable; what it stands for will always be relevant—in every culture, in every age, in every place. For hidden within that simple bottle of oil is the liberating gospel of the Lord Jesus Christ, the message that never grows old.

A CLOSER LOOK AT HEALING

BY MELANIE

As a registered nurse, I spent a good portion of my career fighting to save lives in the intensive care unit. Like most health care professionals, I've seen the inexplicable; a brain dead judge who, after the proof of three flat EEGs (brain wave tests), received a cerebral jump-start from God and not only recovered, but went on to try a staggering number of cases on the federal court circuit.

I witnessed a dead man who, after a long and fruitless resuscitation, drew a deep breath from God, sat up in bed, and described in intricate detail what each of us had done and said during the long labor over his corpse. Not only was his rendition of what happened accurate, but it posed two irrefutable questions for each of us in that room. First, how did a dead man hear what we said? His heart wasn't beating, and he wasn't breathing. In other words, his body wasn't capable of hearing or seeing. If you believe that man is made in the image of God with three parts—spirit, soul, and body—the experience makes sense, because our spirit never dies. The second question that arose in the aftermath of that experience was this: How could a dead man, lying flat in bed with a mask over his nose and mouth and his eyes closed, have seen which of us started his IV and which handled the defibrillator? He explained that his spirit hovered at ceiling height and watched the drama unfold.

For me, perhaps the most poignant turning point in my life happened when I was a very backslidden Baptist in the early years of my career. One of my patients was the picture of a precious saint of God. Small, grey-haired with smile lines around her eyes and gentleness and peace that she wore with dignity even in death. She'd suffered a brain stem stroke and did not respond to stimuli. I happened to be standing beside her bed when the alarm sounded on her heart monitor. I looked up and saw that her heart had stopped. At that very second, I witnessed a miracle, for in the natural what I saw was impossible. Brain dead and with no heartbeat, that saint sat up in bed, opened her eyes, and lifted one hand in the air as though in greeting. I do not have words to describe the rapture on her face or the love that dripped off the word I heard her speak.

"*Jesus!*" she cried, sounding much like a woman who had seen her Lover after a long absence. Every hair on my body stood on end as she closed her eyes and floated back onto the pillow...*gone*. I knew she was gone and that I would never see her again this side of heaven.

I believe the Lord let me witness that extraordinary moment because I'd gotten so immersed in the natural side of life and death that my heart had grown cold to the spiritual side. In the twinkling of an eye, that dear woman passed from one world to the next and God shocked life back into my soul. In a nanosecond of time, I understood that, for all the things we know and see, there are even more that we don't know and can't see except through the eyes of faith.

I mention that experience because death is an integral part of life. It's a door through which each of us will pass if Jesus tarries. Let's face it, heaven is the best of all worlds, which is why the apostle Paul yearned to depart this earth, yet chose to tarry in order to help the young church. I believe that the little lady who welcomed Jesus like a lover would not have stayed earthbound if given a choice.

One of my dear friends has both a mother and a daughter in heaven and in her words, "Heaven is truly sounding sweeter all the time." In my nursing career, I've seen Christians who could have, even in the natural, lived and not died, but the lure of heaven, Jesus, and loved ones on the other side was irresistible. They understood why Paul penned these words in Philippians 1:21, *"For to me, to live is Christ, and to die is gain."*

How wonderful it will be to see Him face-to-face! Just imagine what heaven will be like! No more pain; no tears. No more sickness; no death. Like waves that kiss the shore and then are pulled back into the deep, we have a brief sojourn on earth while being drawn to His eternal presence.

The thing we must remind ourselves is that word *eternal*. We will get to spend eternity with Jesus, but we have only a few brief years to walk this firma terra, to feel the wind in our face, to live and love by faith. So while we're here, let's make the most of every day, and not let the enemy of our souls cut our mission short.

The purpose of this book is not to deny the glory of heaven. It is simply to encourage you to live your life to the fullest, and understand that the anointing to heal is available for you each step along your path.

I must admit that Gina and I have the best jobs in the world. We are God-scribes who have the privilege of testifying about what happens when the prayers of men and the power of God intersect.

We live in the day of satellite news and instant communication via cyberspace, yet God's interaction with man is the single most underreported story on earth. May you be blessed as you think on these things.

PART ONE

STUMBLING INTO THE HEALING POWER OF GOD

BY GINA

Had I known I was about to open the door for a miracle that stifling summer night in 1978, I would have marked the date on my calendar. But I didn't.

As far as I could tell, God wasn't in the miracle business anymore. He'd somehow lost interest in it shortly after the book of Acts was written. I'd heard of occasional exceptions, of course. Everybody does. Now and then it would be rumored that a miracle had happened in Africa or China or some other faraway place. But like most urban myths, such miracles usually happened to somebody's neighbor's friend's uncle's brother-in-law whose exact name no one really knows.

Whether or not such reports were valid, I could not say. But I was fairly sure that if God did decide to perform a miracle in 1978, He would find a more auspicious place to do it than in my little green asphalt-shingled house in San Angelo, Texas. And He would definitely be looking for someone far worthier of that miracle than I.

But then again, it never hurts to ask...and I was desperate. My baby's life was at stake. I had no other choice but to put her into God's hands. All other hands had failed her.

Lifting my daughter's fragile form from her crib, I cradled her as if she might crumble beneath my touch. So perfect, yet so dangerously delicate, she seemed to me like the gossamer globe of a dandelion that at any moment might slip through my fingers and float away in the breeze. In an instant, she could be gone. At nine months old, she weighed far less than she should, not only because of malnutrition but because of dehydration. The skin stretched over her tiny bones was dry and papery. Unlike the spongy, pink flesh of healthy babies, it had no resilience. If I tugged it gently upward to check its condition, it stayed there. If I pressed on it, the indention left by my finger remained.

Ever since we'd brought her home from the hospital as a four-pound premie, I had searched frantically to find some kind of formula or food she could digest. I'd taken her to the doctor again and again. But still, the food wouldn't stay in her stomach. Eventually, the doctors gave up on trying to help her—either because they had exhausted their medical resources or because we had exhausted our financial resources, I will never know which. Either way, the result was the same. My husband and I had been left on our own to figure out how to keep our premature daughter alive.

We'd done everything we knew to do. But what we knew simply wasn't enough.

A jagged sob shoved its way from my heart to my throat as I pressed my lips against the tiny, pale face I'd kissed so many thousands of times during the past few months. Closing my eyes, I blocked out the sight of her hollow cheeks and sunken eyes, and breathed in her sweetness. But I couldn't keep my eyes closed forever. I had to face the truth. The fiery sparkle that had once lit my daughter's eyes was beginning to fade. The nightmare would soon be over.

One way or the other, her endless hours of crying from the pain of hunger would give way to silence. One way or the other, the long nights would end. Nights of walking the floor trying to comfort her, hoping that perhaps tonight she'd keep some milk down and be able to sleep. Nights when the crying would finally stop and I'd stand over her bed holding my breath so I could hear the faint whisper of her breathing and be sure she was still alive.

One way or the other, my little Jennifer would soon find peace. Either the hand of death would take her...or the hand of God would heal her.

I had no right to expect the latter and I knew it. A backslidden Baptist, I'd been straying from God for years, living my own life my own way. Although I'd been raised in church and taught the Bible from the time I was a toddler, in my twenties I'd decided that the God of the Bible and the principles of Scripture were too confining. I'd thrown them off so that I could be free.

As I threw away those principles, I never thought about the promises that accompanied them. It never occurred to me just how desperately I might someday need those promises and the power of the God who made them. That is, until I began to see the little girl I had longed for, the daughter I'd dreamed of since my own childhood, slipping away.

WE DID THE LAST THING WE KNEW TO DO.
WE THREW OURSELVES ON THE MERCY OF GOD.

People sometimes joke about foxhole religions. But when you're actually the one in the foxhole and mortality is staring you in the eyes, you stop laughing. My husband and I found that out for ourselves. As we saw the blossom of our daughter's life withering away, we joined the foxhole faithful and decided to do the last thing we knew to do. The last thing we thought we would ever do. We threw ourselves on the mercy of God.

We had no church to go to, no formal place to make our petition. So we created our own altar of sorts by spreading a baby blanket over the worn gold carpet on our living room floor. In the center of that flannel altar, we placed our daughter. Kneeling beside her, we bowed our heads—something we had never done together before—and prayed.

"Dear God, we have no other hope for our baby. We ask You tonight to heal her and we put her into Your hands. We will trust You because we have nowhere else to put our trust. In Jesus' name, Amen."

ANOINTING FOR HEALING

In Ben Franklin's Footsteps

Sometimes when I think about what happened that night, I'm reminded of old Benjamin Franklin. I think of him waving his key-laden kite hoping to connect with a lightning bolt of heavenly power. A million things could have gone wrong with his experiment. The bolt might have bypassed his key and found a better target. The storm could have blown over before he successfully hoisted his kite aloft. I suppose he even could have electrocuted himself. But, by some happy, divinely ordained accident, Ben Franklin made the power connection.

That night, I too reached out to make a power connection. I hoped against hope that the prayer I waved heavenward might work as well as old Ben's kite did. When the praying was over, I put my tiny daughter into her crib, and, exhausted from the emotion of the evening, I went to bed and fell asleep.

Sometime around 2:00 a.m., I sat upright, slapped awake by the morgue-like silence of the house. For the first time I could remember, Jennifer was not crying. *She's dead!* The thought catapulted me from under the covers and, heart pounding, I bolted from the bed.

But before I took even one step, another thought—one that seemed to come from an entirely different place—apprehended me. *You have put her in God's hands. Leave her there. You can do nothing more for her anyway. Why not just trust Him?*

For reasons I still cannot explain, the idea seemed to make perfect sense. Silently, I slipped back between the sheets. "I trust You, heavenly Father," I said. Then I put my head on my pillow and slept.

When I opened my eyes hours later, my bedroom was drenched with sunshine and the house was still silent. *How late is it?...Oh, no...Dear God, no...*The peaceful trust of the night before had vanished. What had I done? How could I have just left her alone like that? To die alone?

Within seconds I was standing at her bedroom door. Rigid with fear, I stopped. One more step and I would see her lying there in her crib. One more step and I would know how the story had ended. In a kind of deadly anticipation, my skin went cold, and for a moment, I stopped breathing.

Moving to the side of her crib, my eyes swam with tears as I looked down at my silent baby, lying on her back, kicking her feet and smiling up at me in contentment. She was as happy and peaceful as I had ever seen her. She had slept all the way through the night.

From that day on, the food stayed down. The sparkle once stolen from her blue eyes found its way back. Soon, instead of hovering over her in fear, I found myself running to catch her as she dashed across the park, or through the yard, or down the aisle of the grocery store.

For some mysterious reason that I wouldn't understand until years later, God had intervened and worked a miracle. He had healed my little girl.

What Does Oil Have to Do with It?

That was my first experience with *the healing anointing*. Of course, I wouldn't have used that phrase that back then. I wouldn't have been comfortable with it. I thought the *anointing* was just a Bible word that referred to the archaic practice of dabbing oil on somebody's head. I assumed it was something the first century Christians did because they were primitive and didn't know any better.

In the years that have passed since I first encountered it, however, I've discovered that the anointing is much more than that. It is the miracle-working power of the Holy Spirit. It is God's mighty, supernatural ability coming on the scene to do what only God can do. According to the Bible, the anointing is what sets God's people free from the bondage and destruction the devil tries to inflict on them. Isaiah 10:27 puts it this way: *"And it shall come to pass in that day, that his burden shall be taken away from off thy shoulder, and his yoke from off thy neck, and the yoke shall be destroyed because of the anointing"* (KJV).

Based on that verse, one minister I know defines the anointing as God's burden-removing, yoke-destroying power.

It's the power that Jesus operated in when He was on the earth. He said so Himself. At the beginning of His ministry, He declared, *"The Spirit of the LORD is upon Me, because He has anointed Me to preach the gospel to the poor; He has sent Me to heal the brokenhearted, to proclaim liberty to the captives and recovery of sight to the blind, to set at liberty those who are oppressed; to proclaim the acceptable year of the LORD"* (Luke 4:18–19).

> THE PRAYER OF FAITH CONNECTED ME
> WITH THE HEALING ANOINTING OF GOD.

Since oil was used throughout the Old Testament as a symbol of the anointing, the early Christians often used it as a physical sign of the power of the Holy Spirit that is released in response to prayer and faith. That's why the New Testament book of James says, *"Is anyone among you sick? Let him call for the elders of the church, and let them pray over him, anointing him with oil in the name of the Lord. And the prayer of faith will save the sick, and the Lord will raise him up. And if he has committed sins, he will be forgiven"* (James 5:14–15).

According to that verse, it's the prayer of faith, not the oil, that actually saves the sick. I can testify to that because on that amazing night in 1978, I had no anointing oil. Yet somehow I stumbled into the prayer of faith and connected with the healing anointing of God.

You'd think that one miracle would have revolutionized my life. You'd think it would have instantly made a more devoted Christian—if not a towering faith giant—out of me. But according to the Bible, "...*faith comes by hearing, and hearing by the word of God*" (Romans 10:17). It doesn't come just by seeing miracles. Once Jennifer was healed, I left my Bible unopened on my nightstand, so the spiritual spark kindled by God's merciful intervention in my life was soon smothered under the demands of daily living.

I went back to washing dishes, changing my baby's diapers, chasing after my two energetic sons, and cleaning house. As the days marched on marked by nothing so much as their monotonous normality, my miracle, was swallowed up by the mundane details of life.

WHEN LIGHTNING STRIKES TWICE

It's been said that lightning never strikes the same place twice. If that were true, spiritually speaking, I would never have experienced the shock of seeing a miracle again. But I did. In fact, six years later I found myself staring at a veritable stack of them.

Instead of floating down from heaven, as one might imagine miracles should, they were tossed en masse on my desk by the rusty-haired editorial director of the publications department of a major Christian ministry where I'd recently landed a job. "Here's your first assignment," he said, pitching the dog-eared pile of notes and letters my way. "Sort through these testimonies and pick out the best ones. Then call the people who sent them and set up interviews."

Uninspired by the task before me, I sighed and thought about how long it had been since I'd heard someone "give their testimony." I remembered my childhood days in church when people would tell the details about the time they gave their lives to Jesus. Their stories were numbingly similar and usually included an evangelist coming to town to preach a revival, resisting the conviction of the Holy Spirit for the entire week, then walking the aisle on the very last night during the very last chorus of "I Surrender All" and getting saved. *Eat your heart out, Woodward and Bernstein. I get to write about this stuff.*

Despite their lack of dramatic tension, I could appreciate such stories more now than I could then. A few years after Jennifer was healed, I'd finally found out what it meant to surrender all to Jesus. I'd gotten so tired of myself—of my stinking selfishness, my out of control flesh, and my train-wreck of a life—that I'd truly made Him my Lord. In the process, I received the baptism of the Holy Spirit and fell totally in love with God. Although I'd been a writer by profession for years, from then on, all I really cared about was telling people about Jesus. So when I'd gotten an opportunity to go to work for a ministry and write about Him full time, I jumped at it.

My dream job. Yeah, right. Interviewing people about their childhood revival experiences.

Leafing through the envelopes scattered across my desk, one in particular snagged my eye. Scarred and smudged from its long journey, it bore a stack of peculiar, brightly colored stamps in the upper right-hand corner postmarked Haiti. *Haiti?* I thought. *That might be fun. I wonder what revivals are like there.*

Unfolding the letter, I skimmed the contents starting with the signature—Joel Jeune. Highlights...started a

Christian orphanage in Haiti a few years ago...also Christian school...raised from the dead as a child...

What? I caught my breath. *This can't be for real.* I read it again. As well as I can remember now, the letter went something like this:

> ...My father was away from home preaching in the mountains the day I died. By the time he returned, I had been dead for two days. My body already nailed in a casket, the burial was about to take place. My father returned to find the funeral procession carrying me to the cemetery. "Put the coffin down!" he demanded. "The day this boy was born, the Lord told me in a prophecy that he would be a great preacher. God said that he would win many souls here in Haiti and that his ministry would be great. Put him down. God cannot lie!" Then he and the others around him began to pray. Soon they heard a sneeze inside the coffin. When they pried it open, they found me alive.[1]

Stunned, I dropped the letter as if the lunacy that drove this poor, misguided person to write it might somehow be transferred to me. *Well, at least it wasn't boring.*

I set the letter aside and picked up another one. Throwing it down, I picked up another...then another...then another. There wasn't a revival story among them. They were all personal testimonies of people who had been supernaturally healed.

> THEY WERE STORIES OF REAL PEOPLE WHO HAD SEEN GOD WORK REAL MIRACLES IN THEIR LIVES.

Despite my attempt to maintain a sense of journalistic indifference, tears spilled down my cheeks and onto the letters that now lay open on my desk. Since Jennifer's recovery, my only foray into the questionable territory of healing had taken place a just few months earlier when my sister, Susan, had been extremely sick. She was a part of a little Bible study group that had been had meeting at my house. Shortly before she fell ill, our group had recently read and discussed the instructions in James 5:14–15 and we jointly determined we should muster the courage to obey them. We prepared the anointing oil by spritzing some Crisco (the only kind of oil we had) with Heaven Sent perfume. Then, trying to behave with the dignity of spiritual elders, we paraded down the street to Susan's house, clutching our Bibles and our oil bottle.

In truth, we felt more like a gaggle of first graders trying to build a rocket for the school science fair. But we did it anyway. We dabbed oil on my sister's head and prayed in faith for her to be healed by the next morning. Sure enough, she was.

Even so, I'd been afraid to get my hopes up about divine healing. I'd heard for too many years that the day of miracles had passed away...that even if you pray for healing, you probably won't get it because many times (perhaps even most times) it's actually God's will for us to be sick...He may even send the sickness Himself in order to teach us something... you just never know what God is going to do.

Sure, I'd seen a couple of prayers for healing answered. But then, some people wish on falling stars and occasionally those wishes come true. That doesn't mean they should run out and join the First Church of the Falling Stars. A couple of isolated outbreaks of healing wasn't enough to turn me into a faith nut. I had remained guardedly skeptical.

Under the weight of the testimonies I'd just read, however, my skepticism began to crumble. All the hope that had been dammed up inside me through the years poured forth in a torrent of joyful tears. Scooping up the letters, I hugged them to myself. These weren't the writings of liars or lunatics, they were the stories of real people who had seen

God work real miracles in their lives. And there were too many of them to ignore.

SEARCHING THE SCRIPTURES TO FIND THE TRUTH

Enthusiastic as I was about the empirical evidence for healing that had been piled on my desk, I still wasn't willing to run willy-nilly down the theological path the testimonies seemed to point to—no matter how many of them there were. I'd spent too many years being deceived and drawn off course by man-made philosophies based on the experiences, observations, and opinions of human beings. I was determined never to do that again.

A couple of years earlier, I had made a firm decision to base all of my spiritual beliefs only upon the clear teaching of the Bible. There would be no compromise. No adding to or taking away from what the Scriptures themselves said was so.

Since I'd made that decision, my life had blossomed. I'd been more blessed and more peaceful than ever before. So, even though the healing testimonies had inspired me, I pledged to follow the example of the Berean Jews in the book of Acts who heard Paul preach the gospel and *"searched the*

Scriptures daily to find out whether these things were so" (Acts 17:11).

What I discovered not only thrilled and surprised me, it gloriously contradicted many of the things I'd heard about divine healing (or the lack of it) all my life. For example, I'd often been told that when people pray for healing, even if they pray in faith, sometimes God says *no*. I had always assumed that was true. After all, God has the right to do whatever He likes and if He wants to refuse someone's request for healing He can.

The more I studied what the Bible has to say about the matter, the more I realized the very idea is preposterous. The Bible covers six thousand years of God's dealings with mankind, and it doesn't record even one instance when God refused to heal one of His children who reached out to Him in faith. On the contrary, both the Old Testament and the New Testament reveal a God who is willing and able to heal all who call upon Him 100 percent of the time.

What's more, the Bible declares that Jesus is the *"express image"* (Hebrews 1:3) and the perfect reflection of His heavenly Father. He so accurately portrayed the will of God during His earthly ministry that He could say, *"He who has seen Me has seen the Father"* (John 14:9). In light of those statements, I could draw only one conclusion. *If God* reserves the right to refuse healing to some, even though they ask for it in faith, then Jesus would have surely refused to heal at least one person during His earthly ministry.

I scoured the Gospels to find one such incident. But I couldn't. Instead, what I found was that God had anointed Jesus "*with the Holy Spirit and with power, who went about doing good and healing all who were oppressed by the devil*" (Acts 10:38).

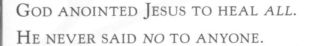

GOD ANOINTED JESUS TO HEAL *ALL*.
HE NEVER SAID *NO* TO ANYONE.

God anointed Jesus to heal *all*. He never said *no* to anyone. When the multitudes came to Him to be healed "*power went out from Him and healed them **all***" (Luke 6:19, emphasis added).

Still, I had questions. Since the healings recorded in the Gospels took place before Jesus went to the cross when He was physically on the earth, I wondered, *Is healing still as available to us today as it was to the people who reached out to Him then?*

Once again, I dove headlong into the Scriptures to find the answer. What I learned was stunning. I found out that healing is not only as available to us today as it was then, it is more available to us today because God included healing in the plan of redemption. People today no longer have to go to a particular location and press through the crowds to touch Jesus' physical body and be healed. They can receive healing the same way they receive the new birth. They can receive it anytime, anywhere, by a simple prayer of faith.

That revelation was a shock to me because I'd always thought that when Jesus was crucified, He only paid the price for the salvation of our souls, not for the healing of our bodies. But the Bible says, "*Surely He has borne our griefs and carried our sorrows…But He was wounded for our transgressions, He was bruised for our iniquities; the chastisement for our peace was upon Him, and by His stripes we are healed*" (Isaiah 53:4–5).

Some people say the healing mentioned in that verse refers to spiritual healing and not physical. But in my studies, I found that same passage quoted in the New Testament in reference to Jesus' *physical* healing of the multitudes. According to Matthew 8:16–17, Jesus "*healed all who were sick, that it might be fulfilled which was spoken by Isaiah the prophet, saying: 'He Himself took our infirmities and bore our sicknesses.'"*

The Bible left no doubt about it. Jesus provided for our spiritual salvation *and* our physical healing at Calvary. Because of what He did, healing belongs to every born-again child of God. Like salvation, it is received by simple faith and therefore comes most easily not to those who are intellectually wise and sophisticated, nor to those who are considered highly spiritual, but to those who will embrace it with childlike humility.

I will always be glad that the majority of the people Jesus healed during His earthly ministry were not great scholars or spiritual giants. They were just ordinary joes, everyday people who believed and spoke and acted like Jesus would heal them. They were regular folks like me.

After a few months of study, the issue was settled for me. The evidence in the Word of God was indisputable. I finally knew beyond any doubt that Jennifer had been healed... and my sister had been healed...not just because of some unexplainable cosmic accident, but because God in His great mercy had, through the sacrifice of His only begotten Son, provided healing—spirit, soul, and body—for all who would receive it by faith. I finally believed that God was willing and able to heal us all.

As Simple as One...Two...Three

When I was a little girl, my mother gave me a cookbook—*Easy Recipes for Kids*, or something like that. I was barely tall enough to see above the kitchen counter at the time. Undaunted by my undersized stature, however, when the mood struck, I would don an oversized apron, open the cookbook, and gleefully set to work cracking eggs, splashing milk, and scooping sugar into a bowl (hopefully in the prescribed proportions).

Never mind that I'd never attempted that particular recipe before. Never mind that I had no idea why the eggs were necessary, or how on earth sliding the whole sloppy mess into a 350 degree oven would transform it into a cake like the one pictured in the cookbook. I didn't need to know all that. I simply had faith in the cookbook and in my mother who had given it to me. As children do, I just believed that the cookbook was telling me the truth and that if I followed the directions in it, I would achieve the desired result.

Thank God, in 1984 when I first discovered the truth about divine healing, I was naive enough to tackle it with the same childlike confidence. I hadn't yet been introduced to the spiritual sages who would one day inform me that there are many complexities involved in healing that I might not understand. God, in His grace, had protected me for a season from the spiritual pundits who profess to know far more about God (yet seem to receive far less from Him) than silly spiritual children who take the Bible literally.

Those folks hadn't gotten to me yet. Instead, I was surrounded with good news. My eyes and ears were filled only with the Word of God and the testimonies of people who had experienced the wonder of divine healing. For a while, all was bliss. I was full of robust faith that, should I ever need healing, I would surely believe for it and receive it.

Of course, when you don't need healing, when you're feeling fine, such confidence is easy to come by. I found that out sometime in October 1985 when reality hit me in the form of a raging internal infection. Assaulted by fever, weakness, and a relentless pain that made every step an exercise in agony, the healing truths I'd learned suddenly seemed more impractical than I had initially believed. Temporarily casting them aside, I rushed to the doctor. He gave me a prescription of powerful antibiotics (a three week course of treatment, as I recall) and told me it might well be several weeks before I saw significant improvement. Since I had a history of such infections, I knew that in purely natural terms his diagnosis was accurate. I went home that evening and took the first pill.

The next day at the office was excruciating, but somehow I hobbled and winced my way through. Winding up my work at five o'clock, I glanced up at the shelf above my desk where my Bible lay unopened next to a book entitled, *God's Will for You Is Healing*, a book by Gloria Copeland, which in its directness and simplicity was much like *Easy Recipes for Kids* in that it provided straightforward directions that were drawn from the Bible and designed to help anyone (even spiritual novices like me) receive healing from God.

WHY DON'T YOU JUST TRUST GOD AND FOLLOW THE INSTRUCTIONS?

The directions went something like this. First: Go to the Bible and find a Scripture that promises you healing and take your stand of faith upon that promise. Second: Confess out loud your faith in that promise. Third: Begin to act as though your healing is already done. Act in faith.

No question about it. That was a good book. Pulling my car keys from my purse, I rose from my chair and headed toward the door when a familiar thought apprehended me.

Why don't you just trust God and follow the instructions?

I stopped, flashing back on the time years before when a very similar question had convinced me to go back to bed and leave my daughter in the hands of God. *Yes, why not?*

Sinking back into my chair, I listened as the sounds of my coworkers gathering their belongings and going home for the day drifted over the bluish gray partitions that formed my office cubicle. Florescent lights flickered then winked out here and there throughout the office. Somewhere an office door clicked shut. That's when I knew if I didn't act on what I'd learned about healing, a divine door would close in my life. I'd lose the revelation and the healing light in my heart would go out.

Just take the first step. Find a Scripture that promises you healing and take your stand of faith upon that promise.

The instant I made my decision, the faith I'd been building over the past few months came roaring to life. I snatched my Bible from the shelf, leafed through the pages and found Psalm 103. Verses 1–3 leaped up at me, shimmering with healing promise.

> *Bless the LORD, O my soul; and all that is within me, bless His holy name! Bless the LORD, O my soul, and forget not all His benefits: Who forgives all your iniquities, Who heals all your diseases.*

From childhood I had been taught that God instantly and fully forgives all the sins of every repentant person who asks for that forgiveness by faith in the blood of Jesus. Believing that was effortless for me. When I did something wrong and asked God to forgive me, it never occurred to me to doubt His forgiveness. I didn't check to see if I felt forgiven, or if I saw any immediate sign of that forgiveness. I just believed God forgave me because the Bible said He would.

I looked again at Psalm 103. It not only said that God forgives all my sins. It said He heals all my diseases. *Why should I believe the first statement and doubt the second? Why should I act as if it were any more difficult to receive healing than it is to receive forgiveness?*

"Heavenly Father," I prayed, "I come before You now by faith in Jesus, trusting in His name and in His blood that was shed for me, because I need healing for this infection in my body. I see in Your Word that to You, forgiveness of sin and physical healing are the same. You have provided them both for me. So I ask You to heal me, and I believe I receive that healing now. I thank You for it, in Jesus' name, Amen."

The fourth chapter of Acts tells about a time when a group of believers in Jerusalem asked God to stretch forth His hand in healing power and the very building shook in answer to their prayer. The building didn't shake when I prayed that day in my bluish gray cubicle. Fire didn't fall. The wind of the Spirit didn't sweep through and blow the papers off my desk. As far as I could tell, nothing happened at all.

According to the instructions in the book, the next thing I needed to do was say out loud that I was healed. So I did exactly that. "I call my body healed in Jesus' name!" I declared confidently to no one in particular.

As my voice faded to silence, I considered the final instruction. *Begin to act like you are healed.* "Lord, I don't know what to do about this one. Exactly how do I act like I'm healed?"

What would you be doing at this time of day if you were healed?

"I'd be running the track at L.D. Bell High School, getting my daily workout."

Then run.

Run? How could I run when just walking around the office had left me breathless with pain? How could I...?

You can do it because you are healed.

Oh yeah, that's right. The pain almost made me forget. I'm supposed to act like I'm healed not because I feel healed but because I believe I am healed. I'm supposed to act in faith.

WHEN HEALING COMES

Some memories fade over the years. But my memory of the first lap around the track that night is as sharp as ever. With every step, jagged shards of pain ripped through my body and one wicked thought jabbed at my mind. *You are not healed!*

"Yes, I am!" I answered, reaching within myself and finding miraculously the grace I needed to take another step.

More pain.

You are not healed! Unlike the comforting thoughts inspired by the Holy Spirit, this one tormented, mocked, and accused. All I knew to do was answer it by faith.

"Yes, I am healed."

You are not!

"Yes, I am."

The argument continued for exactly a quarter mile. One lap around the track. My normal run was three miles. With one lap behind me, I still had eleven to go. Eleven. I couldn't let myself think about it. Instead I forced myself to concentrate only on taking the next step—and on believing that God was faithful...that He could not and would not lie.

I must have experienced at that moment something of what the woman with the issue of blood felt some two thousand years ago when she pushed her way through the crowd that surrounded Jesus, convinced that if she could only touch His clothes she would be healed (Mark 5:28). Admittedly, there were no multitudes on the track blocking the path to my Healer, only a couple of other joggers loping along in the shadows of dusk. But I still had to push my way through to Him.

GOD IS FAITHFUL...
HE CANNOT AND WILL NOT LIE.

Just as that bleeding lady had to push her way through twelve years of doctors trying and failing to cure her, twelve years of negative reports, twelve years of her body testifying day after day of its incurable infirmity...just as she had to push her way through the doubts that tried to block her way, thoughts that screamed through the pain and weakness,

You'll never make it. You'll die before you get to Him. Look how many others are trying and failing to touch Him. What makes you think you'll be the exception? What makes you think you'll get past the obstacles that have stopped everyone else and somehow be the one to get healed?...just like that, I had to push my way through a multitude of memories, pain, and fear to touch the place of true faith.

When the woman with the issue of blood finally reached Jesus, the Bible says that "*immediately the fountain of her blood was dried up, and she felt in her body that she was healed of the affliction*" (Mark 5:29). I know how she felt because that's what happened to me.

There were a few differences, of course. I wasn't standing on a lakeshore in Galilee reaching for the back of Jesus' robe. I wasn't believing that if I could touch Him, I *would be* healed. I was pounding out the second lap on a high school track in Hurst, Texas. And I was believing that Jesus had *already* touched me. I was believing, despite all natural evidence to the contrary, that I *was* healed.

The outcome, however, was the same. I felt, as surely as she did, the healing power of God wash over me. When it did, every trace of pain instantly disappeared. The fever vanished. Every symptom of that infection fled, never to return again.

Healing doesn't always come that way. Sometimes it comes gradually. Most often, it slips in without a single sensation to announce its arrival. But I will be forever grateful that the first time I knowingly reached out to receive my healing by faith in God's Word, He let me actually feel His healing anointing.

It may not sound especially spiritual to say it this way, but that experience turned me into what country folk in my home state of Oklahoma call an *egg-eating hound*. Once such a dog has tasted an egg, it's impossible to keep him out of the hen house. Try as you may to discourage him, he can never forget what it was like to wrap his lips around that white-shelled delicacy. He'll spend the rest of his life trying to dig his way into the chicken coup.

I can sympathize. Once I experienced the sweetness of God's healing power, I knew I'd spend the rest of my life, if that's what it took, learning how to receive it for myself and how to share it with others. As I write this, more than two decades have passed since that night on the track. In those years, I've had some disappointments. I've experienced times of discouragement. I've had questions that weren't always answered.

But I've also seen for myself and interviewed many people who have experienced firsthand the kinds of miracles recorded in the Bible. Their experiences have not only fortified my faith in the healing promises and power of the Lord Jesus Christ, they have taught me a great deal about how to consistently receive healing whenever I need it. They have helped me live for many years in divine health.

When I first began recording the testimonies of those people, I wrote their stories myself. Then the Lord connected me with someone far more gifted at telling those stories than I am. Her name is Melanie Hemry. She and I have been best friends and writing buddies for many years now. We have laughed together and cried together countless hours over the healing stories we have been privileged to hear and record.

You wouldn't have the time to read—nor would she have the time to write—a book containing all of those stories. The volume is simply too great. So she has chosen five sparkling gems to share with you. They are not vague urban myths. They contain real names and dates and places. They are definite, factual accounts of God's healing anointing at work today.

May they bless you as they have blessed us and inspire you to reach out and receive for yourself the healing anointing of God.

PART TWO

...AND JESUS HEALED THEM ALL

BY MELANIE

LIFE IN TECHNICOLOR

Holland was entombed in ice and snow, its vivid springtime colors buried in their watery graves like dead men's bones. Annet Oomen turned from her window with a sigh. The frozen landscape painted a perfect picture of the life she and her family lived within the walls of their own home; it was a stark life in black and white. Whatever girlish dreams she'd had of living a fairy tale when she married and started a family had given way to hard reality. If her life had been a movie, it would have been a horror film.

A scream split the silence and Annet ran as she heard the steady *thump...thump...thump* of four-year-old Desmond beating his head against the wall. She dropped to the floor and wrapped her arms around her son. "It's okay....it's okay," she whispered as she rocked him. "*Shhh...it's all right.*"

But it *wasn't* all right.

Something was dead wrong with their son. At first Annet and her husband, Adrie, thought perhaps they'd been too doting as parents. Had they loved him so much that they failed to teach him how to act? Had they forgotten to teach him boundaries of behavior? He'd always been a difficult baby, but if Desmond's behavior had been a red wagon, the wheels fell off when he was three. He'd stopped communicating with the family; he'd withdrawn into a world where no one else could enter. He wouldn't eat. He wouldn't sleep. He stared into space for hours at a time, or with obsessive compulsions ran in circles, screamed, or beat his head. He spoke primarily in a language all his own, except for the mind-numbing repetition of, "I am Desmond."

Even more frightening, he didn't process pain normally. Once they'd been driving for miles when he murmured a word that sounded similar to "pain." Annet turned to look at him, but he had no expression on his face. She stopped the car and discovered that his little hand had been shut in the door. He didn't cry.

On his fourth birthday, as required in Holland, he started school. Soon after, Desmond's teacher phoned Annet. "Something is very wrong with this child," she said. She refused to allow him back in her class until he'd gone through a six-month battery of tests by health professionals.

Finally they would get answers to their questions.

The doctor who met with Annet and Adrie was one of the top specialists in Europe. She cleared her throat and opened Desmond's file. "Your son has a very serious form of autism," she announced.

Adrie and Annet stared at the doctor without comprehension.

"How do we cure this autism?" Adrie asked, hope lighting his kind face.

"I'm sorry, but there is no cure," the doctor continued. "It's a complex disability that manifests during the first three years of a child's life. We know it's a result of a neurological disorder that affects how the brain functions. Children with autism usually have difficulty in every form of communication and all social interactions. In addition to autism, Desmond has a behavior disturbance and is mentally handicapped.

"We recommend that he attend a special school for children with autism and psychiatric problems. Don't make any plans for his future. The most you can expect is that he might someday get accepted into a special home."

GOD *WANTS* TO HEAL DESMOND AND HE *WILL* HEAL HIM.

Blessing and Cursing

Annet's world tilted off its axis. She remembered the first time she felt him kick in the womb, the first time she heard him cry, and the first time he'd held out his arms to her with absolute certainty that she would fix whatever troubled him. Never had she imagined a world so cruel that her beautiful son would be trapped in a hell from which she could not rescue him.

Although Annet was a Christian, Adrie was not. At church, Annet found comfort, but she did not find answers to the nightmare that was destroying her son's life. Their family was falling apart at the seams from the unrelenting challenge of dealing with Desmond's autism. The stress tore at Annet and Adrie's marriage and affected the younger children. By the time Desmond was seven years old, Annet had lost hope. In despair, she stopped going to church.

In 1996, one of Annet's friends invited her to attend Jubilee, a new church. The pastor's sermon dealt with Deuteronomy 30:19, *"I call heaven and earth as witnesses today against you, that I have set before you life and death, blessing and cursing; therefore choose life, that you and your descendants may live."*

Later, when the pastor heard about Annet's experience with an autistic child, he said, "Well, Annet, you've come to the right place, because God *wants* to heal Desmond and He *will* heal him."

SINGLE-MINDED TENACITY

Weary and heartsore, Annet felt furious that this pastor would offer false hope. Hadn't she lived with an autistic child for eight years? Hadn't she prayed and asked God to heal him? Hadn't dozens of specialists given their expert opinion that there was no hope for Desmond? How dare anyone glibly suggest that God could heal him?

Over the next few days, the words in Deuteronomy 30:19 plagued her. *What if life and death for Desmond hinged on my choices? What if his healing hinged on my not giving up on him? What if it hinged on my not giving up on God?*

Annet took a deep breath and made a hard decision. "Lord," she said, "I'm going to go back to that church. I'm going to do whatever the Bible tells me to do, and I'm going to do everything that the pastor tells me to do."

In addition to attending the church services, Annet signed up to attend their Healing School. Weeks later, she sat with her pastor and sipped a steaming cup of coffee.

"Healing school opened my eyes," she said. "The Bible says that *nothing* is impossible with God. That means no matter how impossible Desmond's situation seems to me, it's not impossible for God.

"I also realized something else. The Bible says that a double-minded man will receive nothing from God, and I've been double-minded. I would pray and ask God to heal Desmond, then talk on the telephone to anyone who called, telling them how awful the situation was. I realize that I not only have to change the way I pray, but I also have to change what I say. I'm going to start speaking God's Word over Desmond, and I'm going to stop spending time with people who don't have faith that God can heal him."

"If you do that," Annet's pastor replied with a smile, "you're going to see a miracle."

A MIRACLE IN YOUR MOUTH

The first witty idea the Lord gave Annet was to lasso Desmond's obsessive compulsive tendencies and use them to his good. After much effort, Annet was able to stop Desmond from repeating hundreds of times a day, "I am Desmond." She got him to change the words to, "I am healed." Day after day and hour after hour, Desmond Oomen said, "I am healed...I am healed...I am healed."

At the market, friends met Annet with sad looks and kind hugs. "How's Desmond, and how are you holding up under the strain?"

Instead of rehearsing the problem, Annet smiled and said, "I'm so happy that Desmond will succeed in life! He is a joy to everyone and can do anything that he desires!"

People couldn't get away from her fast enough, their looks suggesting that perhaps Annet needed psychological help. She refused to speak things over her son that were contrary to what she asked for in prayer. She submerged herself in the Scriptures, in church services, and stayed up late at night watching Christian programming on television.

Nothing changed.

For two years, from 1996 to 1998, Annet refused to look at her circumstances, but set her eyes on God's Word, which says that by Jesus' stripes we *were* healed. She believed that Jesus paid the price for Desmond to be healed of autism on Calvary. She chose to thank God for Desmond's healing although he banged his head and screamed. She praised the Lord for Desmond's healing even though he refused to communicate, he seldom slept, and mealtimes were a form of torture as he spit out his food.

GOD'S VERDICT

"It doesn't matter what I see with my eyes, hear with my ears, or feel with my emotions," Annet told Adrie, "I will never stop believing that God healed Desmond two thousand years ago on Calvary."

It was that kind of tenacity that kept Annet speaking God's verdict over Desmond rather than that of the doctors. No one was more aware of the facts about Desmond's condition than Annet. She didn't deny the facts; she simply believed that the Truth would change them.

Desmond did not exhibit a shred of improvement. There was no gradual change, no slight increase in his attention span. It was an ordinary day when ten-year-old Desmond went, as usual, to the special school for children with autism and psychological disorders. That morning, every symptom of autism was in full bloom. That afternoon he came home and did something he'd never done in his life. He walked up and looked his mother in the eye.

"Mom, can I ask you something?" he said. "Why am I at a school with strange children? They don't talk. They push one another down. They scream..."

Tears streaming down her face, Annet grabbed the phone and called Adrie. "You'd better come home because our miracle has arrived!"

Adrie dropped his tools and sped home. For the first time in his life, he sat down at the kitchen table and had a conversation with his son. Annet couldn't stop weeping; Adrie couldn't stop grinning. Desmond took it all in stride.

When God called Desmond Oomen out of the tomb of autism, it wasn't a partial work. He was so vibrant with life and health that Adrie immediately gave his heart to Jesus, as did Annet's mother, father, and many relatives and friends.

ANNET DIDN'T DENY THE FACTS; SHE SIMPLY BELIEVED THAT THE TRUTH WOULD CHANGE THEM.

THE MASTER'S TOUCH

Adrie and Annet asked the specialist to retest their son. There was no evidence of autism. "He plays well with others," they were told. "He listens well. He communicates well. He is obedient. He has a good grasp of sums. He is one year ahead in his reading level."

There were other changes. Because of his poor balance and motor skills, Desmond had never been able to ride a bicycle or catch a ball. Within weeks he was riding a bike and playing sports.

In April of 1998, Annet and Adrie enrolled ten-year-old Desmond in public school. He went from a classroom of six special needs children to a playground filled with hundreds of boisterous boys and girls. He reveled in it.

"Desmond didn't have any trouble adjusting to a regular school," Annet told reporters who arrived later to interview her. "The only problem was that he'd lived in his own world for so long that he knew nothing about ours. From 1998 to 2000 we taught him things most children already knew: that cars run on gasoline, that you have to pay for groceries, and that florists sell flowers. By the time he was twelve years old, he'd caught up on everything he'd missed."

When he graduated from elementary school, Desmond was admitted to Holland's highest academic program. At 6 foot 5 inches, he is an avid soccer player who excels in sports, academics, and plans on studying law. He is extremely social and filled with joy and good humor.

Spring arrived in Holland this year with a riot of colors; red, green, yellow, and purple tulips splashed the countryside as a vivid reminder that winter never lasts forever. One touch of the Master's brush changed Desmond Oomen's life from black and white to Technicolor. Their home is filled with laughter and their hearts are filled with joy.

The Sound of a Miracle

Colored lights on the Christmas tree cast a warm glow over the room as Anita Siddiki slid onto a piano bench and let her fingers ripple across the cool keys. Outside, snow hung like whipped frosting on tree branches, and Toronto looked as though it had been scrubbed clean and repainted in the colors of winter. Launching into Beethoven's Bagatelle in A minor, Anita closed her eyes and allowed the music to wash over her, basking in its beauty.

Later that day the phone rang and Anita picked up a pen to take a message. For some odd reason, she couldn't get her fingers to form the letter A. *How strange!* Had she practiced too long? Doubtful. While still in high school, Anita had attended the Royal Conservatory earning a degree in music. Back then, she'd practiced at least four hours a day. In all her years as a classical pianist, she'd never fatigued her fingers to the point that she couldn't write. Something was wrong, but she had no idea what it could be. Uneasiness settled over her, but she had more important things on her mind to worry about it. She was pregnant with her first child. However, over the next few weeks, Anita's odd symptoms continued, and she made an appointment with her doctor.

Christmas lights blinked in shop windows on December 24, 1991, as Nasir, Anita's husband, drove her to a clinic. "The left side of your body is weaker than your right side," the doctor explained. "I'm ordering more tests."

The next battery of tests included a spinal tap and an EEG of Anita's brain. Their findings were inconclusive. Doctors felt that a final diagnosis might be made following an MRI, but it couldn't be performed until after the birth of her baby.

A few days later, as Anita and Nasir strolled across the Plaza Mall, Anita collapsed. Her left hand curled into a claw as her entire left side contracted into a seizure. Nasir carried her to the car. Later, the muscles relaxed and the spasms released.

Weeks passed and Nasir flew to London on business. A winter storm swept through Toronto blanketing their home in drifts of snow. Alone in the eerie quiet, Anita listened as the answering machine clicked off and on with each power outage. Shivering, she pulled herself out of bed to check the thermostat. One moment she was walking down the hall, the next moment she fell against the wall. Struggling to right herself, she realized that she couldn't walk without listing to one side. *What was happening?*

Her strange symptoms waxed and waned until May 4, 1992, when Anita's son, Matthew, was born. Afterward, she started losing her eyesight. The problem worsened little by little until her doctor sent her to a neurologist.

"Cover your eye and read this letter," a neurologist instructed.

"Doctor, I can't see the letter," Anita said, sighing. "I can't see the chart. I can't even see you."

"All right, I'm going to walk toward you. Tell me when you can see me."

"I know you're in front of me now. I can't see you, but I smell the orange you had for lunch. Please tell me what's wrong. I can't write. I can't drive. I can't play the piano. I can't take care of my baby. I can't feel the softness of his skin. I can't even *see* my baby!"

"We'll have more answers after the MRI," he said.

At home, Anita ached to see her son. Nasir tucked Matthew into Anita's arms and she turned her head until she glimpsed his face through the pinpoint of her remaining vision. *Matthew!* She tried to stroke his cheek, but she'd lost sensation in her fingers and couldn't feel the softness of his skin.

In November of 1992, the day finally arrived for the long awaited MRI. Afterwards, Anita and Nasir met with the chief of neurology at St. Michael's Hospital. "The test confirmed what we suspected," he said, folding his hands across his chest. "The lesions in your brain and spinal cord are conclusive. You have multiple sclerosis."

The words hit Anita like an assassin's bullets. *Multiple sclerosis!* Time stood still. In slow motion she watched the doctor's mouth continue to move; he spoke as though he hadn't just handed her a life sentence...or was it death?

She forced herself to listen as the neurologist explained that nerves are like electrical cords. The covering around the nerve is called the myelin sheath. In patients with multiple sclerosis, the myelin sheath is worn away leaving nerves exposed. When they touch, it's like two hot electrical wires short-circuiting.

"My dear, what we don't know about this disease is far greater than what we do know," he concluded. "We'll get you a wheelchair and a catheter."

Anita Siddiki was twenty-six years old.

A DIVIDED MIND

Medical science offered Anita no hope; her only hope was in God. Before they married, Nasir had been instantly healed of a fatal case of shingles that had swamped his immune system. Anita wanted the same thing—an immediate healing. Yet, they'd prayed for months and Anita's condition only worsened. Even so, her *not* being healed wasn't an option either of them was willing to entertain.

> MEDICAL SCIENCE OFFERED ANITA NO HOPE; HER ONLY HOPE WAS IN GOD.

Trouble hurled itself at them from every direction. The company Nasir worked for was bought out in a hostile takeover. All the top executives—including Nasir—lost their jobs. With very little money to live on, Nasir scraped together enough to buy healing tapes. He installed a continuous play tape recorder beside their bed so that Anita could hear the Word of God twenty-four hours a day. Nurses arrived daily to help with her care.

ANOINTING FOR HEALING

Nasir also struggled to get both Anita and the baby dressed and to church each Sunday morning. Perched on the front row, Anita couldn't see the pastor. Eventually she was too weak to sit through a service and lay on the back pew. She couldn't raise her arms or lift her hands. She raised her little finger as worship to the Lord.

Losing control of her bodily functions was horrifying, but losing her memory was worse. Raised in Canada, Switzerland, and Greece, Anita spoke English and some German, Greek, and French. Now, sometimes she didn't remember the simplest English word, and her speech was slurred.

By November of 1993, Anita had lost all feeling in the left side of her body. Often her brain sent messages that her leg itched. Unable to feel what she was doing, she clawed holes in her leg. She only realized what she'd done when Nasir noticed that her shoe had filled with blood.

"The Lord has shown me some things," Anita announced one afternoon.

"What's that?" Nasir asked.

"I realized that I've been trying to get healed on your revelation. That won't work. I can't receive my healing through anyone else's revelation. It's got to be *my* revelation to bring about *my* restoration."

"You're right," Nasir said. "What else?"

"I have doctrinal questions that have never been resolved. I was raised in a church that taught the truth about salvation, but they also taught that God makes people sick to teach them a lesson. I was taught that it's *not* always God's will to heal. I was taught that healing passed away with the apostles. And probably the biggest stumbling block to my healing is that my mother died of cancer even though we prayed for her. My head believes that healing is for today, but my heart screams, *then why did my mother die?*

"My heart and my head are divided on the subject, and I know that I'll never receive my healing until I get it settled."

Anita listened to the Bible on tape as she searched for answers. She discovered that there was not a single instance in the Bible where someone came to Jesus to be healed and He failed to heal them. Not one.

One evening Anita shared her most recent revelation. "Jesus paid the price for my healing two thousand years ago!" she said. "I've heard other people say this, but the Lord helped me *get* it! As Christians we understand that salvation was purchased for us on Calvary. We understand that it was purchased for the whole world, but everyone doesn't accept it. Those of us who want to receive it do so with *no proof* except the Bible. That's exactly how healing works! The definition of salvation—*sozo*—isn't just eternity in heaven. It means "to be made whole in every way!" I've seen myself as a sick person trying to get well. But because of Calvary, I am a healed person who is commanding sickness to leave my body."

THERE WAS NOT A SINGLE INSTANCE IN THE BIBLE WHERE SOMEONE CAME TO JESUS TO BE HEALED AND HE FAILED TO HEAL THEM.

The next morning as sunlight filtered through the curtains, Anita announced, "Even though I can't see properly, and I can't lift my legs off the bed, it doesn't change the fact that I was healed two thousand years ago! Even though I can't lift my arms properly, I'm not *going* to be healed, I *am* healed."

That night before she went to sleep Anita said, "If I wake tomorrow and I can't see, feel, speak, move, or stand— I'll believe the Word of God that says I'm healed...no matter what the doctor or my symptoms say."

BATTLEFIELD OF THE MIND

If settling the issue of healing was Anita's first challenge, it wasn't her last. The *real* battle was the war over her mind. She was plagued with disturbing thoughts and images. Anita knew that the Bible says to take every thought captive and bring it into obedience of Christ. It wasn't easy controlling rebel thoughts, but no one could do it for her.

Clouds settled over the cemetery like a shroud as Nasir held Matthew beside an open grave. Anita's father and brothers walked solemnly to their cars. Clods of dirt broke against the polished surface of the casket—her casket!

ANITA DIDN'T JUST WANT TO SURVIVE.
SHE WANTED TO *LIVE* AGAIN.

"No!" Anita said out loud, so weak she couldn't turn over in bed. "I refuse to let my thoughts go there!" Closing her eyes, with great effort, she changed the channel in her mind and forced herself to see a different outcome.

The concert hall is hushed as Anita pours herself into the music. Her fingers skip nimbly up and down the keys, the music arising from her heart and racing out her fingertips to fill every molecule of space with the heavenly sound.

"When I see myself sitting in a wheelchair," Anita told Nasir, "I choose to see myself playing tennis instead. When the devil shows me images of my funeral, I see myself playing classical piano. I see myself running and playing with Matthew."

Anita also knew that she needed a scriptural promise on which to hang her faith. She chose 2 Chronicles 16:12–13, "And in the thirty-ninth year of his reign, Asa became diseased in his feet, and his malady was severe; yet in his disease he did not seek the Lord, but the physicians. So Asa rested with his fathers; he died in the forty-first year of his reign."

Even though King Asa died, that Scripture gave Anita faith to live. One of her confessions became, "So I, Anita, sought You, Lord. Therefore, I, Anita, in the twenty-sixth year of my life will not rest with my mother. I will raise my son. I will walk around the block. I will play tennis."

Anita Siddiki didn't just want to survive. She wanted to live again.

BREAKTHROUGH!

Another part of Anita's healing process was weeding the garden of her heart. She asked the Lord to uncover all unforgiveness, and she forgave everyone who'd hurt her. She repented of judging others, of criticism, and of resentments, all of which sicken the heart and block healing.

God also dealt with natural issues. During prayer, Anita heard the words *amino acids*. Nasir heard the word *protein*. They discovered that the myelin sheath is made up of amino acids, which are the building blocks for protein. Anita supplemented her diet with soy protein drinks and felt raw energy infuse her body.

One morning, Anita blinked as she awoke and realized that her vision had returned. Standing over Matthew's bed, she drank in every detail of his appearance. Through her tears she saw Matthew's face...his eyelashes...his dark hair and tiny fingers.

Even so, Anita's battle didn't end quickly. She immersed herself in the Word of God, made her confessions of faith, and stood against multiple sclerosis for two-and-a-half years. The symptoms gradually decreased in length and severity.

The process was so gradual that she was amazed to finally realize that every symptom had vanished.

The sun felt warm on Anita's cheek in the spring of 1994 as she pushed Matthew's stroller through the park. He squealed with delight as Anita chased him through the soft spring grass. When Nasir arrived home from work, they played a game of tennis. Afterward they rested on a nearby bench.

"If I'd believed my symptoms more than God's Word, I would have missed all this," Anita said. "If I'd put a time limit on God, I would have missed my miracle."

She wouldn't have just missed her miracle; she would have missed her life, her children, her marriage, and her ministry. Satan wanted to steal all of that from her, but two thousand years ago Jesus looked ahead and saw her need. He suffered the scourge of multiple sclerosis on the cross. He paid the price in full.

It's been many years since Anita Siddiki was healed of multiple sclerosis. Since her healing, a second MRI has confirmed what Anita already knew by faith: no lesions remain in her brain or on her spinal cord. Today Anita's fingers dance across the keys of her grand piano as her family gathers around to listen. The notes form in her heart where they begin as praise to God, and then they shoot through the nerves to her fingertips where they are released as sound. Every breath, every morning, every day is a gift. Every note, every movement, every sound is a miracle.

ANOINTING FOR HEALING

LANGUAGE OF LOVE

Renee Demski listened to the roar of unleashed power as living waters cascaded over Niagara Falls, exploding into an eternal dance of rain and mist below. She inhaled the liquid air, soaking in the sights and sounds, allowing herself to be drenched in the awe of a God who expressed Himself in such a magnificent language.

GOD'S POWER IS NEVER IN SHORT SUPPLY, AND HIS MERCIES ARE NEW EVERY MORNING.

Having been born and raised near Niagara Falls, Renee never tired of the raw beauty or the reminder that life always recreates itself, God's power is never in short supply, and His mercies are new every morning.

Renee, her husband, Charlie, and daughter, Jennifer, had lived in a variety of places over the years, but now, as midlife settled over them like a warm sweater, they'd moved back to Niagara Falls. With their daughter, Jennifer, out of the nest, Renee had taken a cue from the energy of the

Falls and recreated her own life. In her mid-forties, with a slower metabolism, she'd been overweight and out of shape. She'd changed her diet to healthy foods, taken up tae bo, and exercised twice a day. Now, five years later, at fifty, Renee was 135 pounds lighter and in excellent physical condition. She'd gone back to college and was earning a degree in computer science.

The next thing on her to-do list was to find a church and reconnect with God in a deeper way. She and Charlie had gotten lax about that over the years, but lately they'd both developed a spiritual hunger. They'd have to do something about that soon.

The last weekend in August 2005 flew by in a blur of activities, and Sunday evening Renee rubbed moisturizer onto her hands and crawled into bed with homework on her mind. Monday morning she climbed out of bed and blinked. Her left eye felt funny. Looking in the mirror, she noticed that it was swollen and puffy. *Maybe a bug bit me*, she thought, blinking a few times with no improvement.

Over the next two weeks the swelling and puffiness increased and Charlie made an appointment for her to see a doctor. He ordered a CT scan and then referred her to a specialist, who saw her weekly. Each week the lump she could feel under her left eyelid had grown. Eventually, in addition to the puffiness, her left eye looked droopy and vision in that eye was blurred.

On November 2, 2005, her doctor performed a biopsy of the growth that appeared to be pushing against her eye and distorting it. He also scraped the bone under her left eyebrow. After the procedure, Renee looked in the mirror and grimaced at the sight. In addition to her other symptoms, now her eye was black and blue from the surgery.

Ten days later, Renee, Charlie, and their daughter, Jennifer, were enjoying a quiet dinner at home when the telephone rang. "Mrs. Demski," her doctor said, "we've gotten the results back from your biopsy. You have a cancerous tumor in the lachrymal gland, which produces tears. This is a very aggressive, fast-spreading type of malignancy, which will spread into your head and kill you quickly. We need to remove the tumor and your eye in the next two weeks."

A DARK PLACE

Renee listened as he droned on, feeling as though she had fallen into an abyss from which she could not recover. "No...no...no...this isn't happening," she said.

Charlie saw all the color drain out of his wife's face and took the telephone. He listened to the physician's report and said, "Before you schedule surgery, we want a second opinion."

Once Charlie hung up the phone, both he and Jennifer comforted Renee, who was sobbing. Tears only streamed out of her right eye, the tumor in her tear gland blocked the flow of tears in her left eye. Soon after, Charlie called Renee's parents who hurried over to comfort her. From that night on, sleep often evaded Renee. When she finally fell into an exhausted sleep, Charlie listened to her whimper, cry, and occasionally scream. It was heartbreaking to hear and even more heartbreaking because there wasn't a single thing he could do.

Renee took a leave of absence from her job and classes and told Charlie, "I need God, and I need Him now!" At the recommendation of some friends, they got online and looked up the service times for Victory Christian Center in Lockport,

New York. The next service was Thursday evening. It was a healing service.

Charlie and Renee looked at one another, hope flaring in their hearts.

"This is *God*," Renee said. Charlie agreed.

On Thursday evening, Charlie and Renee slid into seats and listened to the pastor teach on healing. At the conclusion of the service he said, "There are people here who need healing. If you're one of them, please come forward."

THE ANOINTING OIL

Renee stepped forward and told the pastor about her diagnosis. "All right, I'm going to pray for you based on James 5:14–15, which says, '*Is anyone among you sick? Let him call for the elders of the church, and let them pray over him, anointing him with oil in the name of the Lord. And the prayer of faith will save the sick, and the Lord will raise him up. And if he has committed sins, he will be forgiven.*'"

The pastor anointed Renee with oil and prayed for her to be healed. Afterward he said, "Now that you've been anointed and received prayer, I want you to declare over and over that you are healed. Don't let anything—any doctor's report or symptoms—convince you to say anything else. I also want you to read *Christ the Healer* and meditate on and confess these Scriptures."

That night Renee fell into a deep sleep. She did not whimper, cry, or scream, but rested in the arms of God. The next morning, the first words Renee uttered were, "I am healed."

In the days and weeks that followed, Renee did everything the pastor told her to do. She and Charlie meditated on the Scripture verses and confessed many times a day that she was healed. Renee's daughter, mother, father, siblings, and many other relatives and friends offered support and prayed her healing.

Toward the end of November, she met with an oncologist at Roswell Park Cancer Institute in Buffalo, New York, for a second opinion. Her original doctor had sent the slides of her biopsy to them so that they could do their own testing. The black films of her CT scan were posted on a lighted box and the results of her biopsy were in his hand.

"I can confirm that your original diagnosis was correct," he explained. "Because you live in the U.S., you have choices. First, you can do nothing, but if you make that choice you will die. Second, we can surgically remove your eye along with the tumor. Your third option is chemotherapy. There is a good chance that chemotherapy will shrink the tumor."

EYES OF FIRE

Renee chose the third option and was referred to a chemotherapist. That weekend, she and Charlie drove to Syracuse to visit friends. On Sunday they attended church with them at Abundant Life Christian Center. After the service, they were introduced to Associate Pastors Kelly and Gina Lynnes, who were told of Renee's diagnosis.

"It's important that we pray in accordance to the Word of God," Pastor Gina explained. "There are six of us here and I suggest we pray according to Matthew 18:19–20, which says, *'Again I say to you that if two of you agree on earth concerning anything that they ask, it will be done for them by My Father in heaven. For where two or three are gathered together in My name, I am there in the midst of them.'*

"Before we pray, let's discuss what we want to agree on. I suggest that we agree that you are healed, that you do not have cancer, that the tumor and all cancer cells are gone, that you will keep both of your eyes, and that they will be whole and perfect like the day you were born."

They all agreed, and Gina led them in the prayer. Afterward she grabbed Renee's face and held it between her hands. To Renee, it felt like fire came out of Gina's eyes and into hers with each word. Looking deep into her eyes, Gina said, "I curse every cancer cell that has come against your body, and I command those cells to die in the name of Jesus! The Lord has healed you! You will not lose your eyes! You don't have cancer. You will not lose your vision, for God has restored it."

On the drive home, Renee explained the experience to Charlie. "I've never experienced anything like that," she said.

WITHOUT A TRACE

A week later, Renee's eye was swollen, black and blue, and her vision was blurred when she arrived for her appointment with the chemotherapist. With a puzzled look on his face he said, "Mrs. Demski, we need to run more tests. We don't know what this is."

What does that mean? Both oncologists confirmed my diagnosis!

The following week, Renee went back to see the oncologist. "Mrs. Demski, we're doing more testing on the slides of your biopsy. In fact, we've sent them to different labs around the country to verify our findings."

How strange.

At home, Renee looked in the mirror and saw that her eye looked worse than ever. Her vision was more blurred. The tumor pressed against her eye making it off center. Yet day after day and night after night she confessed, "Christ died so that I might be healed."

And each day the tumor grew.

The week before Christmas, Renee met with her oncologist again. "Mrs. Demski," he said, holding his hands out in a gesture of helplessness, "we can no longer find cancer cells on the slides of your biopsy. We've sent them to other labs and they confirm our findings. I don't understand it, and I want to follow your case for a while."

Tears streamed down one side of Renee's face as she and Charlie drove home. "Charlie, the devil put a timeline on my life, but God stood by His Word and healed me!"

She refused to state the obvious: She didn't *look* healed.

THE DEVIL PUT A TIMELINE ON MY LIFE, BUT GOD STOOD BY HIS WORD AND HEALED ME!

TEARS OF JOY

In March 2006, Charlie phoned home and told Renee to read John 16. Closing her left eye to block out the blurred vision, she read the chapter. When she read the words of Jesus in verses 23 and 24, she wept with joy. *"Most assuredly, I say to you, whatever you ask the Father in My name He will give you. Until now you have asked nothing in My name. Ask, and you will receive, that your joy may be full."*

The Lord had made her joy full. Wiping the tears off her face, Renee froze and then ran to a mirror. *Tears were flowing from her left eye!*

A month later, in mid-April, Renee's vision started to improve. The swelling diminished. The puffiness reduced. By the time she arrived at the oncologist's office for her follow-up visit, the only symptom that remained was a small amount of swelling.

"How do you feel?" the doctor asked.

"Fantastic!"

"Your CT scan looks fine. I want to recheck you in August."

On August 19, 2006, Renee met with the oncologist to get the results of her latest CT scan. The doctor shook her hand and asked her to sit in a chair. He looked straight into Renee's eyes and said, "I don't know what to tell you, Mrs. Demski, except this: You had cancer; now you don't. It was there; now it's gone."

Tears streamed from both of Renee Demski's hazel eyes. "Doctor, this is a miracle from God. He took the cancer from me."

GOD IS MAJESTIC, FILLED WITH POWER, MOTIVATED BY LOVE...AND FAITHFUL TO HEAL.

One year to the month after Renee developed an aggressive form of cancer, she had a documented miracle. In Acts 19:11, the Bible says that God worked unusual miracles by the hands of Paul. Renee Demski's miracle was an unusual one as well, for when the finger of God touched her eye and healed it of cancer, every cancer cell present on the slides from her biopsy died as well. Every lab that checked those slides found the same results. There *had* been cancer cells on them, but not a single cancer cell remained.

Her healed eye was put to the test over the next thirty days. She turned in all her papers, took her exams, and finished her coursework. In May of 2006, she graduated with a bachelor's degree in computer science and minors in criminal justice and computer crime.

Today when Renee Demski looks at Niagara Falls, she sees the wonder of it clearly with both eyes. It is a constant reminder that God is majestic, filled with power, motivated by love...and faithful to heal.

CALL 911...FOR A MIRACLE

Wendy Moore chuckled at the antics of her sixteen-month-old son, Jacob. Flushed from a warm bath, his hair still slightly damp, Jacob squealed and tried to crawl away from her and his pajamas. Wendy dropped to her hands and knees in hot pursuit. "I'm going to get you!" she teased. Jacob laughed so hard he couldn't crawl, flopping over onto his back, a quivering mass of giggles as Wendy loomed above.

Still laughing, Wendy picked up her son and drank in the clean scent of baby shampoo. As a paramedic, her days were filled with trauma and tragedy. But at home with her husband, Steve, and son, Jacob, Wendy basked in a life drenched in love.

"It's time for bed," Wendy said, kissing the top of Jacob's head. "Go pick out a book, and I'll read you a story." Jacob toddled off in search of his favorite book and Wendy gathered her muscles to stand. Nothing happened. Her mind sent the signal, but her legs didn't respond.

Not again!

Just a few weeks ago she'd responded to a car wreck, and when it came time to lift the victim into the ambulance her legs had refused to function. It happened again when she answered a 911 call and couldn't get her legs to navigate the steps leading up to the victim's house. At twenty-six, Wendy was in excellent physical condition.

Something was wrong. Wendy scheduled an appointment with a neurologist who ordered an MRI, an EEG, and took a muscle biopsy of her thigh. "I find nothing clinically wrong," the doctor explained.

He ordered antidepressants.

Months later, in June of 2000, Wendy became pregnant with their second child. By the time she was eight months pregnant, the muscle weakness had become so pervasive that she could no longer squat or stand. Her doctor sent her to the University of Michigan for a neurology workup.

Following the exam, the neurologist said, "Your muscle weakness is so severe we don't think you'll be able to push during delivery. We suggest that you have a planned C-section. Come back after the baby is born, and we'll do more invasive tests."

On March 15, 2001, Wendy gave birth to her second son, Zachary. A few weeks later, on April 27, Wendy's husband and parents accompanied her to the University of Michigan where she endured a battery of tests. Afterward, the family gathered to hear the results.

"You have a disease called ALS, which stands for amyotrophic lateral sclerosis, better known as Lou Gehrig's disease," the doctor explained. "It's a progressive neurodegenerative disease that attacks the motor nerves in the brain and spinal cord. The nerves die, making it impossible for the brain to signal the muscles to move. When the nerves can no longer send impulses to the muscles, the muscles waste away."

Lou Gehrig's Disease. Everyone knew Lou Gehrig died! Tears sheeting down her face, Wendy looked stricken. "Am I going to die?"

"Do you really want to know?" the neurologist asked, sighing.

"My sons are two-and-a-half years and five weeks old! So, yes, I need to know!"

"Fifty percent of the patients diagnosed with this disease live two to five years. You'll be fully disabled soon. I suggest that you go on social security and spend what time you have left with your children."

Suffocating Sadness

Still on maternity leave, Wendy explained to her boss that she might not return to work. At home she tried to enjoy her children, but she felt as though a black shroud had dropped over her blocking light, happiness, and hope. She sobbed day and night. Her first thought every morning and her last thought every night was, *My children won't remember me!*

Doctors prescribed a drug that might prolong her life by three to six months. It cost $700 a month. Grasping for any straw, Wendy took the medication only to have the doctor discontinue it because of its adverse effects on her white blood count.

This disease is from the devil. God has given Wendy lots of promises for healing; the Bible's full of them.

Wendy felt like her last shred of hope had been removed. Worse, one of her father's relatives had died of the same disease. Both families rallied around her with physical and emotional support. What else could they do? The situation was hopeless. They knew from firsthand experience that the symptoms would progress until Wendy began to trip and fall, experience slurred speech, and lose motor control. When the nerves could no longer signal the lungs to breath...she would suffocate.

There was not a single ray of hope on the horizon of Wendy's life until she attended a family gathering. "Wait a minute!" Wendy's Aunt Jan announced, getting everyone's attention. "This isn't God's plan for Wendy's life! This disease is from the devil. God has given Wendy lots of promises for healing; the Bible's full of them. You've just got to learn them."

Jan picked up the phone and called a local Bible school she'd attended. "They're about to start the part on healing!" she said. "Wendy, you need to enroll."

"I'll arrange my schedule so that I can be at home with the kids," Steve offered.

"If you need to learn about healing, so do I," her mother said. "I'll enroll too."

"So will I," her father said.

"So will we!" both of her brothers announced.

BACK TO THE BIBLE

Each week for three hours, Wendy, her parents, and both brothers sat under in-depth teaching from the Word of God. Line upon line, precept upon precept, they learned what the Bible said about healing. Each morning Wendy's dad set the VCR to record Christian shows that taught on faith and healing. Each evening the whole family watched the programs.

"I didn't know that the Bible says that we *were* healed on Calvary," Wendy explained to Steve a few weeks into her classes. "We learned that the full meaning of salvation includes wholeness, health, peace, and prosperity. I'm beginning to feel a glimmer of hope. But here's the thing: we were created in God's image and we have a lot of power in our words. We've got to learn to be very careful about what we say.

"I've also learned that faith without works is dead. If I really believed that I was healed, what would I do? I wouldn't sit home and collect disability. I would go back to work and live my life. So that's exactly what I'm going to do."

Wendy scheduled a meeting with her boss. "I'm coming back to work," she said. "I'm standing on the Word of God that says I'm healed. I don't want a pity party. I expect to pull my weight. If I need help, I'll ask for it." Her boss agreed and asked all the other employees to stand in faith with her. Taking their cues from Wendy, they treated her as though she were healed.

FIGHTING FEAR

After grueling days at work, Wendy went home and did exactly what she'd done before ALS attacked her body. She cooked, cleaned, and took care of her children. But the worst part of the battle wasn't physical; it was mental. Fear stalked her like a relentless foe. It tried to sabotage her sleep and steal her joy.

To fight back, Wendy's family printed pages of healing Scriptures and posted them all over her house. Looking in the mirror each morning, Wendy confessed, "By Jesus' stripes I was healed. No weapon formed against me will prosper." She quoted the Scriptures they posted on her refrigerator and her kitchen window. Wendy's family posted the same Scriptures in their homes and prayed them over her as well.

In spite of their prayers and confessions of faith, Wendy's symptoms progressed to muscle twitching. The first time she tripped and fell, Wendy sat on the ground and sobbed. But she refused to ask for help, and she refused to take time off from work.

"By Jesus' stripes I *am* healed," she said through gritted teeth each time she fell.

Three months after her diagnosis, Wendy returned to the University of Michigan for a follow-up exam. "You've lost some strength, but you're stable," the doctor said after his exam. "How are you coping?"

"We believe that by Jesus' stripes I am healed," Wendy explained. "So I'm back at work full time."

"You're working a forty-hour week?" the doctor asked, his eyebrows rising to his hairline.

"Yes, plus I'm attending Bible school and taking care of my children."

The neurologist looked at Wendy's chart and then back at her. The expression on his face asked the unspoken question. *How?*

FINDING THE WILL OF GOD

Fear reminded Wendy that one member of her family had already died of this disease. It reminded her of all the good Christian people who'd died prematurely. Each time, she responded to the devil the same way Jesus did—with the Word of God.

"*My people are destroyed from lack of knowledge*" (Hosea 4:6), she said. "*Without faith it is impossible to please Him*" (Hebrews 11:6). She meditated on 3 John 1:2, "*Beloved, I wish above all things that you may prosper in all things and be in health just as your souls prosper.*"

"You know," Wendy said to Steve one night as they cleaned the kitchen after dinner, "in the Lord's Prayer, Jesus instructed us to pray for God's will to be done on earth as it is in heaven. There's no sickness in heaven, so it must not be God's will for us to be sick."

Wendy shared her most fervent prayer request with her parents. "I've been praying that my healing would be verified and the doctors would reverse their diagnosis," she explained.

"Wendy, keep your faith in God and not in the doctor's reports," her parents advised. "Remember, it doesn't matter what the doctors say. God has already said that you're healed."

"That's true," Wendy said. "I take comfort in that."

Wendy's one-year checkup proved that she was still stable. "Would you please repeat your original tests?" Wendy's mother asked.

"There's no need," the neurologist explained. "All of Wendy's tests were definitive for ALS. We would never have given her that diagnosis if we weren't positive."

LITTLE BY LITTLE, THE MUSCLE TWITCHING
STOPPED. WENDY STOPPED TRIPPING. SHE
STOPPED FALLING.

Wendy continued her grueling schedule. She and her family persevered speaking and meditating on the Word of God. They kept attending Bible classes and watching Christian programming. They submerged themselves even more deeply in Scripture. A strange thing happened over time. Little by little, the muscle twitching stopped. Wendy stopped tripping. She stopped falling.

A DEFEATED FOE

In August of 2003—more than two years after her original diagnosis—Wendy reported back to the university for her exam. Later, she found a message from them on her answering machine. "You must have an atypical case of ALS. We'd like for you to come back and repeat the original tests."

On October 20, 2003, Wendy endured needles stuck in her back, head, and body. With excruciating pain, electrical currents coursed through the needles to her nerves. She was peppered with questions, probed, and tested. After her ordeal, the entire neurology team stared at her.

"What's going on?" she asked.

"Wendy," the neurologist said, "you don't have ALS. We don't understand what happened. We can still see the original nerve death that was present when we diagnosed you, but your nerves aren't dying anymore."

The nurse sobbed. "I'm so happy for you! We never get to tell people this!"

Wendy's family found her sitting with her head in her lap, sobbing. "Wendy, *what is it?*" her father asked, rushing to her side.

Wendy lifted her head and smiled through her tears.

"I don't have ALS."

The family was so emotional that the medical team left them alone to rejoice. "I've never felt so close to heaven as I do at this moment," Wendy said as her family hugged her and wept. "The presence of God is so tangible that it seems as though the Lord is saying, 'You stood on My Word and now I'm letting you bask in My presence.'"

> YOU STOOD ON MY WORD AND NOW I'M
> LETTING YOU BASK IN MY PRESENCE.

It's been years since Wendy Moore was diagnosed with ALS and doctors at the University of Michigan documented her healing. During those years, Wendy was promoted to 911 supervisor and has immersed herself in family and fun. Wendy is in the grandstands for Jacob and Zachary's football games, wrestling matches, karate classes, and baseball innings. She teases them, reads to them, and hugs them, drinking in their love, enjoying every moment of the life she almost missed.

GRAND SLAM

"Fifteen-love!" Brian Wills called taking a firm grip on the handle of his tennis racquet before sprinting to backhand the ball across the net. Mid-stride, searing pain set his abdomen on fire. *Not again!* Stumbling, he doubled over in pain taking slow, deep breaths as the ball soared past him. He waved his racquet in surrender and limped off the court. In the locker room, he dropped onto a bench and covered his head with a towel.

What was happening to him?

At twenty-two, Brian Wills was living his dream. He'd graduated from Drury College holding the record as the player with the most wins, 121 of them. Now an assistant coach at the University of Richmond, he was on a grueling training schedule for his upcoming trip to Europe to play on the professional circuit.

His doctor said that the off-again on-again bouts of pain were due to overtraining. He'd cut back on his training schedule, made sure he got plenty of rest, and ate right. When the pain continued, he'd gone to see a urologist.

"It must be in your head," the doctor said.

The pain that drove him off the court was not psychological. But as days passed with no recurrences, he made preparations for his flight to Europe in late January 1987. The Friday night before his departure, he woke around midnight with chills, fever, and pain. Saturday morning he went to see the family doctor.

The doctor walked back into the exam room holding Brian's lab work and shaking his head. "Your blood count is alarming," he said. "I'm admitting you to the hospital."

"But my flight leaves tomorrow!"

"I'm sorry, Brian, but you won't be on it."

"Nothing has changed except the date," Brian's parents assured him. "We can reschedule."

Later, the doctor strolled into Brian's hospital room with a frown. "Your right kidney has stopped functioning!" he announced.

One day turned into a week as Brian underwent blood tests, X-rays, CT scans, and a needle biopsy of his abdomen. On the ninth day of his hospitalization, with his family gathered around him, his doctor arrived.

"I have some really bad news," he said. "Brian, you have a mass in your abdomen the size of a golf ball, which has been diagnosed as Burkitt's lymphoma. It's a rare cancer usually found in African children, which progresses very rapidly. There are only three hospitals in the world that treat it. I'm trying to get you into the National Institute of Health in Bethesda, Maryland."

His words seemed to suck all the air out of the room, making it hard to breathe. Brian's mother finally found her voice. "Could we take him home for the weekend to pray?" she asked.

"Yes," the doctor replied, "but I must warn you how fast this tumor grows. It's been known to kill children in a day."

ANOINTING FOR HEALING

Taking a Stand

Silence hung over the room like a shroud when the doctor left. Brian had been raised in a close-knit Christian family. The gospel he'd witnessed as a child wasn't a weak one. He'd seen blind eyes opened. He'd seen the deaf regain their hearing. He'd been instantly healed of many childhood diseases and illness. Along the way, the whole family had learned the power of their words. They all knew that what was spoken next would set their spiritual course.

Brian's mother broke the silence by quoting a well-known Scripture. "*Let God be true but every man a liar*" (Romans 3:4).

"*Let God be true but every man a liar*," they answered with one voice.

Satan had lobbed a deadly threat against Brian's life, and his mother fought back with the Word of God. She walked to the foot of his bed, struggling to choose her words. Speaking from Psalms 118:17, she declared, "Brian, you will live and not die. You will declare the works of the Lord."

Because healing had always come easy for Brian, he left the hospital sure that he would be instantly healed. That night he attended a healing service where he received prayer from a minister known to operate in the gift of miracles. The next day, doubled over in excruciating pain, he went to another healing meeting. By Monday, his abdomen protruded as though he were pregnant.

Too Far Gone

On Tuesday, his parents had to carry him into the National Institute of Health (NIH) for his consultation with one of the world's leading experts on this disease. After his exam the physician shook his head. "I don't think there's anything I can do for you," he said. "You're too far gone."

Too far gone?

The tumor that had been the size of a golf ball on Friday now measured almost ten inches across. The cancer had spread to Brian's liver, lungs, and most of his other organs. The doctor turned to his parents and said, "Today is Tuesday, and your son won't be alive on Friday. I'll admit him to the hospital and keep him as comfortable as possible."

When the doctor stepped out of the room to make the necessary arrangements, Brian's mother said, "No, God's Word says that by Jesus' stripes Brian is healed. Let God be true and every man a liar."

"*Let God be true but every man a liar,*" they agreed.

Brian was admitted to a ward of incurable patients at the NIH. The only way anyone left was by way of the morgue. Everyone, including Brian's roommate, talked incessantly about their disease, their diagnosis, their prognosis, and what their doctors said. They were dying like flies caught in an early frost.

The Lord spoke to Brian and said, "*Son, if you allow yourself to think the way they're thinking, and speak the way they're speaking, you'll get the results they're getting.*"

GOD'S WORD SAYS THAT BY JESUS' STRIPES BRIAN IS HEALED. LET GOD BE TRUE AND EVERY MAN A LIAR.

THE COUNTDOWN

The nurses measured the mass in his abdomen regularly as it completed its death march across his vital organs. That evening, the doctor returned with results of the latest tests. "Your right kidney hasn't worked for weeks, and your left one won't be able to function much longer. Your cancer is growing by the hour."

The doctor talked with Brian's father alone in the hallway. "I give Brian ten hours or less to live."

Brian looked out the window. *Ten hours! I'll never set foot outside this hospital. I'll never again feel the wind on my face. I'll never play the European circuit. I'll never play another game of tennis. I wonder what my dog will think when I don't come home.*

When his parents followed the doctor into the hall, Brian prayed a foxhole prayer. "Lord, I've seen You heal all my life. I don't know what's going on, but I commit my life to You now. I'll go wherever You want me to go; I'll do whatever You want me to do."

"*Son, I Am your healer. I will manifest healing to you as you take the steps I tell you to take.*"

For the first time, Brian understood that he had a part to play in the process. "What's the first step, Lord?"

"*Forgive.*"

Brian saw a person's face from his past and knew he must be harboring unforgiveness in his heart. "Lord, I don't know how to reach them," he said.

A phone number floated up from the recesses of his mind. That evening, he dialed the number and that person answered. Brian asked for forgiveness, never mentioning that he was on his deathbed.

BRIAN KNEW THAT HE'D RECEIVED TWO MIRACLES. HIS KIDNEY STARTED FUNCTIONING. AND HE WAS ALIVE.

Within hours, his right kidney started working.

When sunlight streamed through the hospital window, Brian knew that he'd received two miracles. His kidney started functioning. And he was alive.

Each time the Lord brought names and situations to Brian's mind, he remembered the words of the Lord's Prayer,

"*Forgive us our sins, just as we have forgiven those who have sinned against us*" (Matthew 6:12 TLB). Brian understood that because God had forgiven his sins, he must forgive others. For the next two days he repented of every sin and offense the Lord brought to his mind.

GOD SEALS THE DEAL

None of the doctors could understand why he was still alive. They assumed it was taking longer for him to die because he was in such excellent physical condition.

Having repented, Brian asked for the next step. The Lord reminded him of Malachi 3:8–11 where God promised to rebuke the devourer for His Old Testament people if they would give Him a tenth of their income. As a New Testament believer, Brian had always tithed as an expression of his love of God. Only out of college a few months, Brian hadn't tithed on his income. He calculated the amount and asked his parents to draw it out of his account and give it to the church.

Over the next few days, Brian's condition improved. His kidneys continued to function. The mass in his abdomen decreased in size. The pain subsided. He lived.

Because of his improvement, the doctor ordered a CT scan and a pre-dose of chemotherapy. "It won't help you," he explained, "but it will let us know how you react to it."

That evening, the doctor came back to Brian's room with the report. "We don't understand what's happening with you," he said, a perplexed look on his face. "The radiologist said they checked you head to toe three times and you were NED."

Heart hammering in his ears, Brian asked, "What's NED?"

"It means there is no evidence of disease. There's no tumor in your abdomen. There's no cancer in your liver, lungs, kidneys—none of your organs. There's no trace of Burkitt's lymphoma in your body. And we have no explanation."

THE PROTOCOL

Laughing, Brian turned to his mother. *"Let God be true but every man a liar!"*

"Let God be true but every man a liar!" she agreed, laughing and wiping away tears at the same time. Brian felt like he'd been on the receiving end of a firing squad whose guns failed.

He was packing his belongings when several doctors arrived. "We want you to proceed with chemotherapy," they urged.

"You said yourself that I have no evidence of disease," Brian retorted. "Why would you recommend chemotherapy?"

"That's right, you have no evidence of disease, but if even one cell is left somewhere in your body it could come back. We've decided that you should stay and get treated with our new chemotherapy—protocol MB-204."

Brian and his family agreed to stay. It was a decision they would question many times over the coming months.

Brian's family plastered his walls with computer printouts of healing Scriptures. They put the Scriptures on three-by-five cards and agreed to pray over every pill and every dose of medicine that went into his body. They played Scriptures on tape and praise music twenty-four hours a day.

Two weeks into chemotherapy, Brian reacted violently. Spasms of nausea racked his body, and he couldn't keep anything down. He lost strength at an alarming rate. Shivering under the covers, he heard his mother say, "Brian, it's time to speak the Word." Between bouts of nausea he declared the Scriptures.

Weeks later, Brian's temperature soared to 105. "That's high enough to fry an egg," the nurse said, "and it could fry your brain." She packed him in ice blankets.

"What's wrong with me?" Brian asked, his teeth chattering with chills.

"The chemotherapy has wiped out your immune system," she explained. "That's why you get infections so easily. You've got *Candida*. Most people die within hours when they have it as bad as you do."

As her voiced droned on with horror story after horror story, Brian turned his face to the wall and read the words silently, too sick to speak out loud. *"Then Jesus went about all the cities and villages, teaching...preaching...and healing every sickness and every disease among the people"* (Matthew 9:35).

A Double Dose

In his third week of the *Candida* infection, Brian's temperature still soared as he lay packed in ice. "I'm so sick, Mom," Brian said. "I can't even speak the Scriptures." She wrapped her arms around his wasted frame and they both wept.

That night the Lord reminded Brian of Proverbs 4:20–22, "*My son, give attention to my words; incline your ear to my sayings. Do not let them depart from your eyes; keep them in the midst of your heart; for they are life to those who find them, and health to all their flesh.*"

The next morning, Brian explained the revelation to his dad, who'd arrived for his weekly three day vigil at Brian's bedside. "I'm getting enough of the Word of God in me to stay alive in spite of this infection," he said. "But I'm not getting enough in me to kick it. Somehow I've got to double up on Scripture. God's Word is medicine to my flesh, but the chemotherapy is stripping me of life. So I've got to find the strength to ingest more Word."

Brian upped his dose of the Word, spending two-and-a-half hours a day confessing Scriptures one thousand times. In addition, he started reading two extra chapters of the

Bible. In spite of that, his hair fell out by the handfuls, and he lost forty pounds.

Each of his roommates died. But Brian Wills did not die.

Almost eight months after he was admitted to the NIH, a mere shadow of his former self, he was discharged. "If you survive the next three months without a recurrence, it will probably never return," his doctor explained. "If that happens, you need to understand that you'll never be able to have children, as the chemo has rendered you sterile."

At his six-month checkup, the doctors gave Brian some startling news. "The chemotherapy we gave you had never been tested," they said. "We've since discovered that the drugs themselves were lethal. Every person ever treated with protocol MB-204 died...except you."

Brian Wills received two miracles. First he was healed of cancer. And then God healed him of the poisonous effects of the chemotherapy. God allowed him to live his dream and play tennis on the European circuit. It's been many years since Brian was healed of Burkitt's lymphoma, and he kept his promise to God. A minister of the gospel, he travels all over the world teaching, preaching, and praying for the sick.

If that weren't enough, Brian and his wife, Beth, are the proud parents of four children.

That's not just a win; it's a Grand Slam.

PART THREE

NOW IT'S YOUR TURN

BY GINA

As inspiring as it is to read about others who have been divinely healed, God never intended any of us to be satisfied with someone else's story. He wants us all to taste for ourselves the sweetness of His healing anointing. He wants every believer to have a story of their own.

Granted, that's sometimes hard to believe when we gaze across the landscape of the church and see so many suffering believers bowed down like lilies in a drought for lack of healing rain. Scattered among them, as we have seen, are desert flowers who have tapped into the waters of God's healing anointing and thrived. But sometimes even those bright blossoms pale beside the memorials of those who prayed earnestly for healing...and never received it.

Why didn't those people get healed?

That's a crucial question. It's the question that almost sealed Anita Siddiki in a tomb of multiple sclerosis. It's a question so common that in all my years of teaching and ministering healing, I've never met anyone who didn't struggle with it. Unlike Anita, many people ultimately let it quench the fire of their faith. They answer it by diluting the truths of the Bible to fit the experiences of people who failed to see those truths borne out in their lives. That is always a tragic mistake. It is always wrong to allow one person's failure to receive the fulfillment of God's promise to cast doubt upon the promise itself.

God always means what He says. He always keeps His promises. If He gives His Word, He honors it without fail. Even though He is almighty and sovereign, He has in His sovereignty chosen to bind Himself to His Word. Even though as God He has the undeniable right to change His mind, where His Word is concerned, He will never do it. *"You have magnified Your Word above all Your name"* (Psalm 138:2).

GOD WANTS EVERY BELIEVER TO HAVE A STORY OF THEIR OWN.

That being so, one might well ask how we explain it when the experiences of good people—*God's people!*—don't appear to line up with the Bible? There's only one wise way to respond to that question. We must draw the answer directly from God Himself. He says, *"My people are destroyed for lack of knowledge"* (Hosea 4:6). Or, as Jesus put it in John 8:32, "*You shall know the truth, and the truth shall make you free.*"

If the truth we know will make us free, it stands to reason that not knowing that truth will leave us in bondage. So it has been for many Christians. They have been bound by sickness—not because God willed it, not because by suffering with it they would somehow glorify God (a totally unscriptural concept!)—but because they didn't fully grasp with all their heart the truth about divine healing. Or, having once grasped it, they couldn't hold on when the going got tough. Perhaps no one around them knew how to stand with them and encourage their fledgling faith like Wendy Moore's family encouraged hers when she was facing Lou Gehrig's disease. Perhaps they had no one to study God's Word with them like she did, no parents or brothers like hers who could stand with them staring contrary symptoms in the eye while still declaring, "We believe that by Jesus' stripes you were healed." Perhaps they just didn't know what to do when the lies and doubts of the devil assailed them so they lost their grip and let their healing slip away.

Most of us have known such folk, and if we haven't known them we have most certainly heard others rehearse their experiences. "Sister Sally and brother Bill were the most saintly Christians I've ever seen. They prayed for healing and died anyway." What a tragedy such stories are sometimes used to slap the fingers of eager believers who reach out for divine healing! What a shame they are scattered like weed-seeds of doubt into the hearts of Christians who are trying to cultivate faith to receive!

I sometimes wonder what saintly sister Sally and brother Bill think of such stories. Now that they are leaning over the banister of heaven as a part of that great cloud of witnesses, they must be thoroughly dismayed to see their life experiences used to cast doubt upon the clear teaching of God's Word. Now that they are standing in the full light of divine revelation, they must want to shout at us, "Stop it! Stop using my story to discourage people from believing for healing. There were things I missed. Things I didn't understand. Things that are none of your business. Quit focusing on what happened to me and keep your eyes fixed on God's Word. It's the truth!"

I don't really know if they are saying such things. But I do know this. There's only one way for us to truly honor the memory of Sally and Bill and all those like them who somehow had their healing stolen from them. We can finish the fight they began. We can learn how to receive the healing Jesus paid such a price to secure for us. We can honor them by doing what they endeavored to do themselves—rise up and be healed in Jesus' name.

THE DAY THE TUMOR FELL OFF

It doesn't take a rocket scientist to do it. In fact, those who get intellectual about it usually mess it up. During my years ministering in healing school, I saw that proven again and again. New Christians received their healing most easily. They didn't question God's Word or try to figure everything out. In childlike simplicity, they just trusted God to do what the Bible said he would do. No wonder Jesus said:

> *Let the little children come to Me, and do not forbid them; for of such is the kingdom of God. Assuredly, I say to you, whoever does not receive the kingdom of God as a little child will by no means enter it.*
>
> (Luke 18:16–17)

Of course, we don't have to be new Christians or literal, physical children to approach God's Word with that kind of simplicity. My own mother did it at sixty after she'd been teaching Sunday classes and Bible studies for decades. She knew the Scriptures better than most people ever will, but the full truth about divine healing had always escaped her.

When she finally caught the revelation of it, however, she didn't hesitate. She acted on it right away. With the determination of a child taking her first step, she zeroed in on a target—a bothersome but benign tumor that had been growing on her leg for some months. The doctors had warned it must eventually be cut off, but they'd postponed the surgery as long as possible, knowing it would leave her leg severely scarred.

New Christians received their healing most easily. They just trusted God to do what the Bible said He would do.

Laying her hand on the growth, she asked God to confirm the healing truth she had seen in His Word and expected Him to do it. A few days later, the growth withered, turned black, and fell off. It left no scar.

Just so you know this is no urban myth. My mother's name is Helen. She lives in Tulsa, Oklahoma. Although the incident with the tumor was her first experience with divine healing, it was definitely not her last. She is now over eighty-five, and the last time I visited her, she kept me traipsing around Southland Mall with her until I was totally exhausted. She can still outshop me. If you ever go to that mall and run into her, I'm sure she'll be more than happy to tell you the story herself about the day the tumor fell off.

A Matter of the Heart

Maybe you already have the kind of childlike faith that makes it easy to believe and act on whatever the Bible says. But if, like most of us, you're still working on it, here's a secret that will help you. Such faith flourishes best in a heart that is given to God. It comes most easily to those who are not just Christians in name or in doctrine but to those who have entrusted their lives to the Lordship of Jesus Christ.

The Bible says God is always looking to bless such people. It says His eyes *"run to and fro throughout the whole earth, to show himself strong in the behalf of them whose heart is perfect toward him"* (2 Chronicles 16:9).

I can almost hear what you're thinking. *A perfect heart! Dear heavens, I'll never be able to have a perfect heart!*

Yes, you can. In fact, if you've made Jesus your Lord, you already have one.

That's right. If you are a born-again child of God, you already have a perfect heart, and no devil in hell can take it away from you.

That fact staggers the minds of many Christians. They have long thought that the taint of sin has forever ruined them. But they're mistaken. The New Testament says that when we receive Jesus as Lord and Savior, our hearts are washed clean by His blood and our spirit is made absolutely perfect—as perfect as God Himself. It says that *"if anyone is in Christ, he is a new creation; old things have passed away; behold, all things have become new....For [God] made Him who knew no sin to be sin for us, that we might become the righteousness of God in Him"* (2 Corinthians 5:17, 21).

> ### FAITH FLOURISHES BEST IN A HEART THAT IS GIVEN TO GOD.

All of us who want to receive healing need to understand that. Otherwise, the crooked devil will short-circuit our faith with feelings of condemnation and inadequacy. Rubbing our noses in our outward faults and shortcomings, he'll make us ashamed to *"come boldly before the throne of grace, that we may obtain mercy and find grace to help in time of need"* (Hebrews 4:16). He'll convince us we're unworthy of it.

The next time he tries that on you, remember what the Bible says. You are worthy because Jesus Christ has made you so. He has recreated your heart and made it as pure as His own. Sure, you mess up sometimes and make mistakes; but God looks past all that into your heart that has been born again in His image. Like a mother who cherishes a child that has stumbled into a mud puddle, God sees past the outward grime that sometimes clings to us and gazes with delight on our spirit that has been made flawlessly righteous by the blood of His firstborn Son.

> *For the Lord does not see as man sees; for man looks at the outward appearance, but the LORD looks at the heart.* (1 Samuel 16:7)

That does not mean, of course, that as believers we can knowingly misbehave and disobey God with impunity. When we do wrong, we must repent and make it right. Otherwise, our hearts will condemn us and we'll find it difficult even to face God—much less receive healing from His hand.

Whenever I consider what it's like to feel that kind of faith-destroying condemnation, I'm reminded of the anecdote my friend, Henry Clarke, tells about his family's enormous grey Weimaraner named Genevieve. She once fell prey to the canine version of such condemnation because of a cake that was left sitting on the kitchen counter overnight. For several hours Genevieve wrestled with temptation. But sometime in the wee hours of the morning, the aroma overwhelmed her and, knowing full well she was violating the rules of the house, she plunged snout first into the frosting.

The Bible says that it is possible to enjoy the pleasures of sin for a season (see Hebrews 11:25) and, no doubt, Genevieve can affirm that. She smacked her chops over that cake until it was laid bare of every last trace of icing. But sin has its wages, and when Henry stumbled into the kitchen the next morning to make a pot of coffee, Genevieve knew that payday had come.

Finding the cake cover askew and the frosting gone missing, Henry knew immediately who to look for. "Genevieve! Genevieve, come!"

Of course, she didn't come. Because of her transgression, she didn't have the boldness to go before her master. Her heart was condemning her, so to speak, and Henry had to search her out. He found her cringing beneath the dining room table, shivering and ashamed, the very picture of unrighteousness.

Needless to say, if Genevieve had needed something from Henry at that moment—say, a bone or morning romp in the park—she would have found it well nigh impossible to believe for it until she repented. She could have no confidence toward Henry until she rolled on her back and groveled on the floor and did whatever else dogs do to relieve their guilty conscience. Only then could she once again hold her beautiful silver-grey head high and enjoy her master's presence.

IF WE'LL ASK HIM, GOD WILL SPEAK TO OUR HEARTS.

So it is for us when we have committed some sin or held on to some wrong attitude—such as unforgiveness—that we know full well goes contrary to the Word and will of God. Unlike Genevieve, we don't have to roll on our back or grovel in any way, but we do have to acknowledge to the Lord we've done wrong, repent (or change direction), and receive His forgiveness.

Henry never said, but my hunch is that regardless of Genevieve's repentance, he banished her to the doghouse for a while after she hoovered the top off the cake. God isn't like that. He doesn't keep us in the doghouse for even a split

ANOINTING FOR HEALING

second. He always receives us with open arms. *"If we confess our sins, He is faithful and just to forgive us our sins and to cleanse us from all unrighteousness"* (1 John 1:9).

God will not for one moment withhold healing from us because of some sin in our past. Indeed, it's too late for Him to do so! He has already extended healing to every one of His children and He has pledged not to withdraw it because the price for it was fully paid two thousand years ago when Jesus bore our sicknesses and carried our diseases. That's why 1 Peter 2:24 declares in the past tense that by His stripes we *were* healed.

Even so, however, sin can still get in our way. It can stop us from receiving what God has already provided because when we sin and fail to repent, our consciences condemn us. They make our faith feeble. Therefore, instead of pulling up a chair to our Father's table and partaking of the healing provision He has prepared for us, we end up cringing beneath it unable to believe and receive.

Sometimes we're not even aware we've slipped into such a lowly position. But if we'll ask Him, God will show us. He'll speak to our hearts as He did to Brian Wills during his ten-hour cancer battle and say, *Forgive.* Or He'll bring to our minds, ever so kindly, any wrong we need to make right.

When He does, obeying Him is always gloriously simple. All we must do to correct the situation is repent, confess our sins to God, and receive forgiveness and cleansing through the blood of Jesus. Then, by the grace He so generously supplies, we can make the necessary changes and walk uprightly once again before Him. Our hearts will no longer condemn us, and…

Beloved, if our heart does not condemn us, we have confidence toward God. And whatever we ask we receive from Him, because we keep His commandments and do those things that are pleasing in His sight. (1 John 3:21–22)

Of Teeth and Turnips

"If that's the case," you might ask, "why do we still struggle at times to receive healing even when we are wholeheartedly obeying God?"

Often it's because we don't realize just how fervently God desires to give us whatever we ask of Him. We don't fully understand the goodness of God.

Ever since the Garden of Eden, the devil has been trying to steal that revelation from people. Ever since the beginning, he's been lying to them about God's nature. He started out by suggesting to Adam and Eve that God didn't really have their best interest at heart. He poisoned their perspective with his serpentine insinuation that their Beloved Creator was holding out on them by commanding them not to eat of the tree of the knowledge of good and evil. *"For God knows that in the day you eat of it your eyes will be opened, and you will be like God"* (Genesis 3:5).

As we all know, the lie worked. Adam and Eve bought it. So it's no great surprise that the devil is still peddling the same old lie today. If he can't convince Christians that God has gone completely out of the healing business, he'll give them the impression that, although it is available, healing is rare and difficult to come by; that getting God to give it to you is, to use a couple of phrases from my childhood, like pulling teeth or squeezing blood from a turnip.

I admit those terms don't sound very spiritual. Obviously, I didn't draw them directly from the Bible. But had the Bible been written in America a couple of decades ago instead of in the Middle East several thousand years ago, I suspect those phrases might have been included because they communicate so well. They vividly depict the difficulty involved in pushing somebody into doing something it is not their nature to do. Pulling teeth is hard because the gums are generally reluctant to release them. Squeezing blood from a turnip is impossible because turnips don't have any blood in them. They just have turnip juice, and no matter how hard you squeeze them, barring a miracle, that's all you will ever get.

The devil has tricked all too many people—good, Christian people—into thinking that getting healing from God is like teeth and turnips. It's usually hard...and often impossible. But nothing, absolutely nothing, could be farther from the truth.

God is, by His very nature, a Healer. He demonstrates that throughout the Bible. He even incorporated healing into His own name by calling Himself *Jehovah Rapha*, "*the LORD*

ANOINTING FOR HEALING

who heals you" (Exodus 15:26). Since the Bible declares that God never changes (see Malachi 3:6), if God was the Lord who healed His people thousands of years ago, He is still *the Lord who heals you* today.

GOD IS, BY HIS VERY NATURE, A HEALER.

Of course, under the Old Covenant before Jesus came, it was more difficult for God's people to receive His healing anointing. Because of their fallen nature, they kept cutting themselves off from it by getting bound up in sin. But even so, God kept offering it to them. He kept saying:

- *"You shall serve the LORD your God, and He will bless your bread and your water. And I will take sickness away from the midst of you"* (Exodus 23:25).

- *"You shall be blessed above all people; there shall not be a male or female barren among you or among your livestock. And the LORD will take away from you all sickness, and will afflict you with none of the terrible diseases of Egypt which you have known"* (Deuteronomy 7:14–15).

- *"Do not be wise in your own eyes; fear the* LORD *and depart from evil. It will be health to your flesh, and strength to your bones"* (Proverbs 3:7–8).

- *"Behold, I will bring...health and healing; I will heal* [My people] *and reveal to them the abundance of peace and truth"* (Jeremiah 33:6).

Even when God's Old Testament people rebelled and opened the door to sickness with their own stubborn hands, He rescued them if they repented and reached out to Him for help. Psalm 107 says, they were *"fools, because of their transgression, and because of their iniquities, were afflicted. Their soul abhorred all manner of food, and they drew near to the gates of death. Then they cried out to the Lord in their trouble, and He saved them out of their distresses. He sent His word and healed them, and delivered them from their destructions"* (verses 17–20).

Sometimes God even healed them all simultaneously. When the Israelites exited Egypt, for example, He *"brought* them out with silver and gold, and there was none feeble among His tribes" (Psalm 105:37). When the multitudes of Jews and Israelites gathered to observe the Passover and honor the re-opening of the Temple and King Hezekiah prayed for them, "the LORD listened to Hezekiah and healed the people" (2 Chronicles 30:20).

HEALING RADIATES FROM GOD AND ATTACHES ITSELF TO ANYONE WHO DRAWS NEAR HIM IN AN ATTITUDE OF FAITH.

Indeed, according to the Bible, God is quite literally an easy touch when it comes to healing. He is so full of compassion and healing power that it radiates from Him and attaches itself to anyone who draws near Him in an attitude of faith. I will never forget the lightning flash of His love that shot through me the day I was privileged to pray for Renee Demski to be healed of the tumor on her eye. At that moment, I knew not only because the Bible said so but because I felt it, how fiercely God desires to heal His suffering children. Looking into her frightened eyes, I sensed surging through me a wave of the divine healing ocean whose fathomless depths could easily heal the whole world, and whose tides will sweep over anyone who will stand in faith upon its shores.

I knew then that it's impossible for God to be reluctant to release His healing power. He literally overflows with the lifeblood of healing. It so permeates His nature that if we will only get close to Him and believe, we will be drenched by its mighty flow.

That's not just poetic imagery, either. It's the Bible. It's what happened consistently in the ministry of Jesus. *"Wherever He entered into villages, cities, or in the country, they laid the sick in the marketplaces, and begged Him that they might just touch the hem of His garment. And as many as touched Him were made well"* (Mark 6:56).

ANOINTING FOR HEALING

How to Cultivate the Touch of Faith

As the folk who lived in Nazareth a couple of thousand years ago proved, however, it is the touch of faith not the touch of doubt that makes the healing connection. When Jesus went to minister to them, *"He could do no mighty work there, except that He laid His hands on a few sick people and healed them. And He marveled because of their unbelief"* (Mark 6:5–6).

It wasn't that Jesus *wouldn't* do any mighty works for the people in Nazareth. It's that He *couldn't*. Their unbelief insulated them from the effects of His love and power. Of course, Jesus reached out to them anyway and scrounged up a few folk He could heal even in that hard-hearted crowd. That's just the way Jesus is. He abounds in mercy, just like His heavenly Father.

Still, He prefers to minister to people who have faith because He can get healing to them every time. During His earthly ministry, He demonstrated that again and again. For instance:

- When the Roman centurion asked for his servant to be healed, Jesus said, *"'as you have* believed, so let it be done for you.' And his servant was healed that same hour" (Matthew 8:13).

- When the four friends of the paralyzed man brought him to Jesus to be healed, "*Jesus saw their faith....Then He said to the paralytic, 'Arise, take up your bed, and go to your house'*" (Matthew 9:2, 6).

- When the woman with the issue of blood touched His garment, Jesus said, "*Be of good cheer, daughter; your faith has made you well*" (Matthew 9:22).

WE CULTIVATE THE FAITH FOR HEALING BY HEARING...AND HEARING THE WORD OF GOD.

- When two blind men cried out to receive their sight, "*Jesus said to them, 'Do you believe that I am able to do this?' They said to Him, 'Yes, Lord.' Then He touched their eyes, saying, 'According to your faith let it be to you'*" (Matthew 9:28–29).

- When the Gentile woman begged Jesus to heal her demon-possessed daughter, *"Jesus answered and said to her, 'O woman, great is your faith! Let it be to you as you desire.' And her daughter was healed from that very hour"* (Matthew 15:28).

- When the father asked if Jesus could heal his epileptic son, Jesus said to him, *"If you can believe, all things are possible to him who believes"* (Mark 9:23). Then, after healing the boy, Jesus turned to his disciples who had asked why they were unable to help the child themselves, and He said, *"Because of your unbelief; for assuredly, I say to you, if you have faith as a mustard seed, you will say to this mountain, 'Move from here to there,' and it will move; and nothing shall be impossible to you"* (Matthew 17:20).

- When one of the lepers Jesus healed came back to thank Him, Jesus said to him, *"Your faith has made you well"* (Luke 17:19).

How do we cultivate the kind of faith for healing these people had? By hearing...and hearing the Word of God (see

Romans 10:17). By reading it and listening to it. By thinking about it and fellowshipping with the Lord over it in prayer.

According to Jesus, God's Word is actually spiritual seed. When it's planted in the soil of our heart, if we don't allow the lies of the devil or the pressure of natural circumstances to steal our confidence in it, it will always grow up and produce faith. (See Mark 4:1–29.) Always. It may not grow instantly, but it will grow if we stick with the process.

It will come up as surely as the carrot seed I once buried in the crusty soil of my west Texas garden. Much like the Word, that seed proved it could overcome great obstacles to bear fruit. Obstacles like me. Ignorant of the basics of agriculture, I planted it far too deep, and I was disappointed when harvest time came and went with no carrots in sight.

A year passed. Then two. By that time, I'd abandoned my attempt at gardening and seeded over the site of my ill-fated carrot patch with Bermuda grass. Imagine my surprise then when one day as I padded barefoot through that grass lugging a bag of trash to the garbage can I stubbed my toe on a carrot top!

Bless its gnarly orange heart, that carrot was so committed to fulfilling its purpose, it labored away for two years unseen and unappreciated in the dark Texas dirt. And, despite my mistakes, it eventually broke through to the light of day and produced a harvest. Overcoming all obstacles, it did what it was divinely designed to do.

If a carrot seed can accomplish such a feat, just think what the supernatural seed of God's Word can do. Unlike natural seed that decays over time, the Word of God is incorruptible seed *"which lives and abides forever"* (1 Peter 1:23). So even when planted imperfectly, if it is kept in the ground of our heart, it will eventually grow up and bear the fruit of faith. Jesus assured us of it. He said:

> *The kingdom of God is as if a man should scatter seed on the ground, and should sleep by night and rise by day, and the seed should sprout and grow, he himself does not know how. For the earth yields crops by itself: first the blade, then the head, after that the full grain in the head. But when the grain ripens, immediately he puts in the sickle, because the harvest has come.* (Mark 4:26–29)

Annet Oomen believed those words and acted them. Despite two years with no sign of a harvest, she refused to give up on the seed of God's Word. And because that seed never fails, her son, Desmond, eventually broke through the blackness of autism and is living life in Technicolor today.

Taking Our Responsibility

No doubt, we would see more such miracles if more believers understood how to do what Annet Oomen did. But most don't even know they should. They're like the minister I once heard about who dropped by to visit a farmer that lived near his church. Settling themselves in a pair of rocking chairs, the two sat together on the front porch for a while studying the lush crops that blanketed the surrounding land.

Finally, the minister broke the silence. "God certainly did give you a beautiful farm, didn't He?" he said.

The wizened codger pondered his answer for a moment. "God did give it to me," he acknowledged, "I'll grant you that—and it's a good thing He did, too. You should have seen the sorry shape it was in when He was working it by Himself."

Good point. That farmer understood something many Christians do not. He realized that God doesn't work on the earth apart from man. Certainly *the earth is the Lord's, and all its fullness, the world and those who dwell therein* (Psalm 24:1). Certainly God created it and owns it. But He leased it to mankind when He made Adam and said, "*Let Us* make man in Our image, according to Our likeness; let them have dominion over...the earth" (Genesis 1:26). With that one statement, God placed the responsibility for cultivating the earth firmly into human hands.

Psalm 115:16 says it this way, "*The heaven, even the heavens, are the Lord's; but the earth He has given to the children of men.*"

That's why people who let their Bible gather dust on the coffee table and leave their healing solely "in God's hands" rarely experience His healing anointing. That's why very few people are supernaturally healed when they passively say, "If it's God's will, He'll heal me. If it's not, He won't. The will of the Lord be done."

What would happen to the farmer's land if he left it exclusively in God's hands? What kind of crops would he have if he never rolled up his sleeves and planted seed? What kind of harvest would he have if he just said, "Well, if it's the Lord's will for crops to grow in this land, they'll grow. If not, they won't."

That kind of farmer would go not only go broke, he'd end up claiming God was the One who broke him!

Jesus didn't teach us to have that kind of attitude. When He talked about spiritual farming, He didn't say that God

Himself would plant the Word in our hearts while we surf the Internet and watch television. He said, "*The kingdom of God is as if a man should scatter seed on the ground*" (Mark 4:26). The man must plant the seed himself. In other words, planting isn't God's responsibility; it's ours. We are the ones who initiate the process and we do it by obeying the instructions God gives us in Proverbs 4:20–23:

> *My son, give attention to my words; incline your ear to my sayings. Do not let them depart from your eyes; keep them in the midst of your heart; for they are life to those who find them, and health to all their flesh. Keep your heart with all diligence, for out of it spring the issues of life.*

When we do that, God's mighty power is released within us and the seed of His Word grows up and bears fruit. We don't have to make it grow; God will see to that. He will make sure that the Word we plant produces a harvest of faith.

When that harvest comes, however, if we want to reap the fruits of it, we must once again take action. We must, as Jesus said, immediately put in the sickle. (See Mark 4:29.)

BELIEVE, SPEAK, AND ACT

Although I didn't realize it at the time, that's exactly what I did back in 1986 when I was healed of that internal infection while running the track. I harvested the faith that had been growing in my heart from my study of the Word. And I did it with three simple steps.

First, I took my stand on a scriptural promise and prayed the prayer of faith. I followed the instructions Jesus gave in Mark 11:22–24 where He said:

> Have faith in God. For assuredly, I say to you, whoever says to this mountain, "Be removed and be cast into the sea," and does not doubt in his heart, but believes that those things he says will be done, he will have whatever he says. Therefore I say to you, whatever things you ask when you pray, believe that you receive them, and you will have them.

When I asked God to heal me that day, I didn't just hope He would do it. I didn't wait to see if the symptoms improved before trusting that God had kept His Word to me. I believed I received my healing *when I prayed* and I chose to continue believing despite contrary evidence. I chose to believe God's

Word was more trustworthy than anything else—including the painful testimony of my physical body.

God said if I believed I received my healing when I prayed that I would be healed. So I believed it. Period. Symptoms or no symptoms.

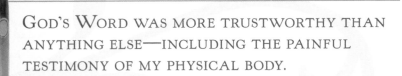

GOD'S WORD WAS MORE TRUSTWORTHY THAN ANYTHING ELSE—INCLUDING THE PAINFUL TESTIMONY OF MY PHYSICAL BODY.

The second thing I did was speak by faith. And why not? According to Jesus, *"whoever says...but believes that those things he says will be done....Whatever things you ask when you pray...you will have them."* Obviously, when it comes to releasing our faith, what we say is very important. Second Corinthians 4:13 confirms that. It indicates that our words provide evidence of our faith and declares: *"'I believed and therefore I spoke,' we also believe and therefore speak."*

No wonder God tells us to *"let the redeemed of the LORD say so, whom He has redeemed from the hand of the enemy"* (Psalm 107:2); and Proverbs 18:21 tells us that *"death and*

ANOINTING FOR HEALING

life are in the power of the tongue, and those who love it will eat its fruit."

God Himself *"calls those things which do not exist as though they did"* (Romans 4:17) and wants His people to do likewise. One of the first folks who really caught on to that concept was Abraham. When he was far too old to father children and married to a ninety-year-old, barren woman, God told Abraham to call himself *the father of many nations.* So he did.

> *And not being weak in faith, he did not consider his own body, already dead (since he was about a hundred years old), and the deadness of Sarah's womb. He did not waver at the promise of God through unbelief, but was strengthened in faith, giving glory to God, and being fully convinced that what He had promised He was also able to perform.*
> (Romans 4:19–21)

The night I received my first healing by faith, I dared to copy Abraham's example. I declared that what the Bible said about me was true. I said, "By the stripes of Jesus I am healed."

The third and final thing I did to reap my harvest was to act in faith. The Bible says, *"Faith without works is dead*" (James 2:20). Just as crops left in the field too long will eventually die, faith not expressed in action will lose its potency. That's why Jesus told the man with the withered hand to stretch it forth before there was any evidence the hand had been healed. It's why He told the ten lepers who asked for healing to go show themselves to the priests and verify their healing before they saw any change in their bodies. "*And so it was that as they went, they were cleansed*" (Luke 17:14).

I don't know why faith actions connect us with the healing anointing of God. I just know the Bible says they do. And I proved it myself that night when I ran the first lap by faith. Even though it hurt, God gave me the strength to do it and when I did, everything changed.

BELIEVE, SPEAK, AND ACT. GOD'S WORD HAS NEVER FAILED ME.

YOUR STORY

Believe, speak, and act. If I had done those things and received divine healing as a result only once or twice in my life, I wouldn't have written this. But it hasn't been just once or twice. I've done it more times than I can remember now, and God's Word has never failed me. As a result, I haven't gone to the doctor for sickness in fifteen years. Make no mistake about it, I believe good doctors are a great blessing, and I would have sought their help if I needed it...but I haven't. Whenever I have personally needed healing, Jesus has met my need every time.

Even better, I've discovered that a continual diet of God's healing promises can have a wonderful preventative effect. Each day during my prayer time I declare a few of the healing Scriptures—those which the Holy Spirit seems to be quickening to me at the time—and thank Jesus for being my Healer. I purposely release my faith that as my Great Physician, He will keep me well. The more I have done that, the healthier I've become.

I've heard that in some Asian countries, doctors are paid most highly not to cure disease but to prevent it. I like that concept and, apparently, the Lord is agreeable to it as well because years often come and go now without my experiencing any symptoms of sickness. On the rare occasions they do crop up, they disappear within days.

But that's my story.

Now, it's time for yours. So plant the Word, let it grow, and reap the harvest. Then go share the good news that God hasn't retired from the miracle business. He is alive and as active as He ever was. In Jesus' name, by the anointing of His Spirit, He is healing His people today.

HEALING
SCRIPTURES

TAKEN FROM THE
NEW KING JAMES
TRANSLATION

"So Abraham prayed to God; and God healed Abimelech, his wife, and his female servants. Then they bore children" (Genesis 20:17).

"If you diligently heed the voice of the LORD your God and do what is right in His sight, give ear to His commandments and keep all His statutes, I will put none of the diseases on you which I have brought on the Egyptians. For I am the LORD who heals you" (Exodus 15:26).

"So you shall serve the LORD your God, and He will bless your bread and your water. And I will take sickness away from the midst of you" (Exodus 23:25).

"And the LORD will take away from you all sickness, and will afflict you with none of the terrible diseases of Egypt which you have known, but will lay them on all those who hate you" (Deuteronomy 7:15).

"Bless the LORD, O my soul; and all that is within me, bless His holy name! Bless the LORD, O my soul, and forget not all His benefits: who forgives all your iniquities, who heals all your diseases, who redeems your life from destruction, who crowns you with lovingkindness and tender mercies, who satisfies your mouth with good things, so that your youth is renewed like the eagle's" (Psalm 103:1–5).

"He sent His word and healed them, and delivered them from their destructions" (Psalm 107:20).

"Trust in the LORD with all your heart, and lean not on your own understanding; in all your ways acknowledge Him, and He shall direct your paths. Do not be wise in your own eyes; fear the LORD and depart from evil. It will be health to your flesh, and strength to your bones" (Proverbs 3:5–8).

"My son, give attention to my words; incline your ear to my sayings. Do not let them depart from your eyes; keep them in the midst of your heart; for they are life to those who find them, and health to all their flesh" (Proverbs 4:20–22).

"But He was wounded for our transgressions, He was bruised for our iniquities; the chastisement for our peace was upon Him, and by His stripes we are healed" (Isaiah 53:5).

"For thus says the High and Lofty One who inhabits eternity, whose name is Holy: 'I dwell in the high and holy place, with him who has a contrite and humble spirit, to revive the spirit of the humble, and to revive the heart of the contrite ones.... I have seen his ways, and will heal him; I will also lead him, and restore comforts to him and to his mourners'" (Isaiah 57:15, 18).

"And Jesus went about all Galilee, teaching in their synagogues, preaching the gospel of the kingdom, and healing all kinds of sickness and all kinds of disease among the people" (Matthew 4:23).

"When He had come down from the mountain, great multitudes followed Him. And behold, a leper came and worshiped Him, saying, 'Lord, if You are willing, You can make me clean.' Then Jesus put out His hand and touched him, saying, 'I am willing; be cleansed.' Immediately his leprosy was cleansed" (Matthew 8:1–3).

"Now when Jesus had come into Peter's house, He saw his wife's mother lying sick with a fever. So He touched her hand, and the fever left her. And she arose and served them" (Matthew 8:14–15).

"When evening had come, they brought to Him many who were demon-possessed. And He cast out the spirits with a word, and healed all who were sick, that it might be fulfilled which was spoken by Isaiah the prophet, saying: 'He Himself took our infirmities and bore our sicknesses'" (Matthew 8:16–17).

"But when Jesus knew it, He withdrew from there. And great multitudes followed Him, and He healed them all" (Matthew 12:15).

"Then great multitudes came to Him, having with them the lame, blind, mute, maimed, and many others; and they laid them down at Jesus' feet, and He healed them" (Matthew 15:30).

"Then the blind and the lame came to Him in the temple, and He healed them" (Matthew 21:14).

"Now a certain woman had a flow of blood for twelve years, and had suffered many things from many physicians. She had spent all that she had and was no better, but rather grew worse. When she heard about Jesus, she came behind Him in the crowd and touched His garment. For she said, 'If only I may touch His clothes, I shall be made well.' Immediately the fountain of her blood was dried up, and she felt in her body that she was healed of the affliction" (Mark 5:25–28).

"And when they came out of the boat, immediately the people recognized Him, ran through that whole surrounding region, and began to carry about on beds those who were sick to wherever they heard He was. Wherever He entered into villages, cities, or in the country, they laid the sick in the marketplaces, and begged Him that they might just touch the hem of His garment. And as many as touched Him were made well" (Mark 7:54–56).

"Then they brought to Him one who was deaf and had an impediment in his speech, and they begged Him to put His hand on him. And He took him aside from the multitude, and put His fingers in his ears, and He spat and touched his tongue. Then, looking up to heaven, He sighed, and said to him, 'Ephphatha,' that is, 'Be opened.' Immediately his ears were opened, and the impediment of his tongue was loosed, and he spoke plainly" (Mark 7:32–35).

"Then He came to Bethsaida; and they brought a blind man to Him, and begged Him to touch him. So He took the blind man by the hand and led him out of the town. And when He had spit on his eyes and put His hands on him, He asked him if he saw anything. And he looked up and said, 'I see men like trees, walking.' Then He put His hands on his eyes again and made him look up. And he was restored and saw everyone clearly" (Mark 8:22–25).

"And these signs will follow those who believe: In My name they will cast out demons; they will speak with new tongues; they will take up serpents; and if they drink anything deadly, it will by no means hurt them; they will lay hands on the sick, and they will recover" (Mark 16:17–18).

"When the sun was setting, all those who had any that were sick with various diseases brought them to Him; and He laid His hands on every one of them and healed them" (Luke 4:40).

"However, the report went around concerning Him all the more; and great multitudes came together to hear, and to be healed by Him of their infirmities" (Luke 5:15).

"Now it happened on a certain day, as He was teaching, that there were Pharisees and teachers of the law sitting by, who had come out of every town of Galilee, Judea, and Jerusalem. And the power of the Lord was present to heal them" (Luke 5:17).

"Now it happened on another Sabbath, also, that He entered the synagogue and taught. And a man was there whose right hand was withered. So the scribes and Pharisees watched Him closely, whether He would heal on the Sabbath, that they might find an accusation against Him. But He knew their thoughts, and said to the man who had the withered hand, 'Arise and stand here.' And he arose and stood. Then Jesus said to them, 'I will ask you one thing: Is it lawful on the Sabbath to do good or to do evil, to save life or to destroy?' And when He had looked around at them all, He said to the man, 'Stretch out your hand.' And he did so, and his hand was restored as whole as the other" (Luke 6:6–10).

"And the whole multitude sought to touch Him, for power went out from Him and healed them all" (Luke 6:19).

"Then He called His twelve disciples together and gave them power and authority over all demons, and to cure diseases. He sent them to preach the kingdom of God and to heal the sick" (Luke 9:1–2).

"Now He was teaching in one of the synagogues on the Sabbath. And behold, there was a woman who had a spirit of infirmity eighteen years, and was bent over and could in no way raise herself up. But when Jesus saw her, He called her to Him and said to her, 'Woman, you are loosed from your infirmity.' And He laid His hands on her, and immediately she was made straight, and glorified God" (Luke 13:10–13).

"Now a certain man was there who had an infirmity thirty-eight years. When Jesus saw him lying there, and knew that he already had been in that condition a long time, He said to him, 'Do you want to be made well?' The sick man answered Him, 'Sir, I have no man to put me into the pool when the water is stirred up; but while I am coming, another steps down before me.' Jesus said to him, 'Rise, take up your bed and walk.' And immediately the man was made well, took up his bed, and walked. And that day was the Sabbath" (John 5:5–8).

"Now as Jesus passed by, He saw a man who was blind from birth. And His disciples asked Him, saying, 'Rabbi, who

sinned, this man or his parents, that he was born blind?'
Jesus answered, 'Neither this man nor his parents sinned,
but that the works of God should be revealed in him. I must
work the works of Him who sent Me while it is day; the
night is coming when no one can work. As long as I am in
the world, I am the light of the world.' When He had said
these things, He spat on the ground and made clay with the
saliva; and He anointed the eyes of the blind man with the
clay. And He said to him, 'Go, wash in the pool of Siloam'
(which is translated, Sent). So he went and washed, and
came back seeing" (John 9:1–7).

"And believers were increasingly added to the Lord,
multitudes of both men and women, so that they brought
the sick out into the streets and laid them on beds and
couches, that at least the shadow of Peter passing by might
fall on some of them. Also a multitude gathered from the
surrounding cities to Jerusalem, bringing sick people and
those who were tormented by unclean spirits, and they were
all healed" (Acts 5:14–16).

"Now it came to pass, as Peter went through all parts of the
country, that he also came down to the saints who dwelt in
Lydda. There he found a certain man named Aeneas, who
had been bedridden eight years and was paralyzed. And
Peter said to him, 'Aeneas, Jesus the Christ heals you. Arise
and make your bed.' Then he arose immediately" (Acts
9:32–34).

"God anointed Jesus of Nazareth with the Holy Spirit and with power, who went about doing good and healing all who were oppressed by the devil, for God was with Him" (Acts 10:38).

"And in Lystra a certain man without strength in his feet was sitting, a cripple from his mother's womb, who had never walked. This man heard Paul speaking. Paul, observing him intently and seeing that he had faith to be healed, said with a loud voice, 'Stand up straight on your feet!' And he leaped and walked" (Acts 14:8–10).

"And it happened that the father of Publius lay sick of a fever and dysentery. Paul went in to him and prayed, and he laid his hands on him and healed him. So when this was done, the rest of those on the island who had diseases also came and were healed" (Acts 28:8–9).

"But if the Spirit of Him who raised Jesus from the dead dwells in you, He who raised Christ from the dead will also give life to your mortal bodies through His Spirit who dwells in you" (Romans 8:11).

"Now may the God of peace Himself sanctify you completely; and may your whole spirit, soul, and body be preserved blameless at the coming of our Lord Jesus Christ" (1 Thessalonians 5:23).

"Is anyone among you sick? Let him call for the elders of the church, and let them pray over him, anointing him with oil in the name of the Lord. And the prayer of faith will save the sick, and the Lord will raise him up. And if he has committed sins, he will be forgiven. Confess your trespasses to one another, and pray for one another, that you may be healed. The effective, fervent prayer of a righteous man avails much" (James 5:14–16).

"Who Himself bore our sins in His own body on the tree, that we, having died to sins, might live for righteousness; by whose stripes you were healed" (1 Peter 2:24).

"Beloved, I pray that you may prosper in all things and be in health, just as your soul prospers" (3 John 1:2).

ABOUT THE AUTHORS

MELANIE HEMRY

A former intensive care nurse, Melanie Hemry traded in her stethoscope for a computer and now writes poignant true life stories, many of which are set in intensive care. A winner of the coveted *Guideposts* Writing Contest, Melanie's stories have warmed the hearts of readers around the world. She holds a bachelor of science in nursing from the University of Central Oklahoma and a master's degree in Practical Ministry from Wagner Leadership Institute in Colorado Springs. She is also the author of *A Healing Touch: The Power of Prayer*.

Melanie can be reached at melaniehemry.com.

ABOUT THE AUTHORS

GINA LYNNES

A writer by trade and a minister at heart, Gina Lynnes has been a Bible teacher and associate pastor since 1996, ministering especially on the subject of prayer in churches both in the Unites States and abroad. A recipient of the National Religious Broadcasters award for her writing of the *UpReach!* Radio broadcast, she has been involved in Christian publishing for more than twenty years, working behind the scenes as a writer and editor for a number of international ministries. Gina and her husband founded Lynnes Ministries in 2001, and spend their time ministering in Colorado, where they now reside, and in churches across the country.

She can be reached at lynnesministries.com.

keychains & jewelry

oil holders

Biblically Inspired Products for an Anointed Life!

candles

bath & spa